W9-BZI-416

Nathan D. Mitchell

Eucharist as Sacrament of Initiation

LTP

Liturgy Training Publications
in cooperation with

The North American Forum on the Catechumenate

Acknowledgments

The *Forum Essay* series is a cooperative effort of The North American Forum on the Catechumenate and Liturgy Training Publications. The purpose of this series is to provide a forum for exploring issues emerging from the implementation of the order of Christian initiation and from the renewal of the practice of reconciliation in the Roman Catholic Church.

Other titles in the series:

The Role of the Assembly in Christian Initiation
Catherine Vincie

On the Rite of Election
Rita Ferrone (Summer 1994)

Preaching and Christian Initiation
J. Michael Joncas (Winter 1995)

Forum Essays was designed by Mary Bowers and typeset in Futura and Bembo style by Mark Hollopeter. The cover photograph is by Vicky Grayland. Editorial assistance was provided by Sarah Huck, Jennifer McGeary and Maria Leonard. Editors for the series are Victoria M. Tufano (Liturgy Training Publications) and Thomas H. Morris (The North American Forum on the Catechumenate).

Copyright © 1994, Archdiocese of Chicago: Liturgy Training Publications, 1800 North Hermitage Avenue, Chicago IL 60622-1101; 1-800-933-1800, FAX 1-800-933-7094. All rights reserved.

Printed in the United States of America.

Library of Congress Cataloging-in-Publication Data

Mitchell, Nathan.
Eucharist as sacrament of initiation/Nathan Mitchell.
154 p. — (Forum essays; no. 2)
Includes bibliographical references.
ISBN 1-56854-088-6 (pbk.): $6.00
1. Lord's Supper—Catholic Church. 2. Lord's Supper—Doctrines.
3. Initiation rites—Religious aspects—Catholic Church.
4. Catholic Church—Liturgy. I. Title. II. Series.
BX2215.2.M55 1994
234'.163—dc20   93-46859
                                                            CIP

CONTENTS

▪

▪

▪

■

Preface

■

This little book is about the eucharist as that act which completes the sacraments of Christian initiation. Its focus, then, is not upon the whole range of eucharistic theology or doctrine, but upon the meaning of the neophyte's participation in the paschal meal in light of the conversion that leads to baptismal birth and the mystagogy that follows it.

Chapter one seeks to situate the human and religious reality of table companionship within the context of Jesus' life and ministry. It argues that Jesus' call to conversion, a call couched in the provocative language of parable, is a call to come to the table. It asks: What is the path we take to arrive at that "table of dreams" which Jesus linked to the reign of God and which Christians connect with the death of Jesus?

Chapter two looks at the ways Jesus' subversive style of table fellowship re-created the world of human relationships and redefined the religious and cultural significance of dining. It argues that a distinctive feature of Jesus' approach to meals was his insistence upon inclusivity and egalitarianism, his willingness to eat *anything* with *anyone* at *any time.* It asks: Has our emphasis on the Last Supper as a supreme model for eucharistic theology and practice blinded us to the meaning of those meals where Jesus multiplies loaves and fishes in generous, compassionate response to human need?

Chapter three directs attention to the eucharistic theology embedded in—or implied by—the *Rite of Christian Initiation of Adults,* with its emphasis on the intersections between ecclesiology and eucharist, Easter and eucharist. It argues that the church's liturgy presupposes—and requires— a recovery of the "liturgy of the world," a renewal of vision, and a recommitment to the hospitable welcoming of strangers that connects Christian community with the structures of public life. It asks: How do we come to recognize that the mystery of the table is *our own* mystery, that the Lord's Body is not only *on* the table but *at* the table?

Throughout the book my indebtedness to the work of John Dominic Crossan and Thomas Sheehan will be evident. Their stimulating studies of Jesus' life—and its reshaping by the New Testament writers—has had an enormous influence on my own efforts to understand the uniqueness of Jesus' eucharistic teaching.

Invitation to the Dance

■

The Great Dance does not wait to be perfect until all the peoples of our planet are gathered into it. It has already begun! The dance that we dance is at the center, and for the dance all things were made. Blessed be God!

Never did God make two things the same. Never did God utter the same word twice. After *earths,* not better earths, but *beasts.* After beasts, not better beasts, but *spirits.* After a falling, not a recovery, but *a new creation.* Out of the new creation, not a third, but the mode of change itself is changed for ever. Blessed be God!

All which is not itself the Great Dance was made in order that God might come down into it. In the Fallen World God prepared and became a body—was united with the Dust and made it glorious for ever! This is the end and final cause of all creating, and the sin whereby it came is called "Fortunate" *(O felix culpa!)* and the world where this was enacted is the center of all worlds. Blessed be God!

3

The Tree was planted in that world but its fruit has ripened in this. The fountain that sprang with mingled blood and life in the Dark World flows here with life only. . . . This is the Morning Star promised to those who conquer. This is the center of all worlds. Blessed be God!

Each thing was made for God. God is the center. Because we are with God, each of us is at the center. In God's city, all things are made for each. When the Holy One died in the Wounded World, it was not a death for "humanity in general"—it was a death for *each* and *every* individual person. If each person had been the only one alive, God would have done no less. Each thing, from the single grain of sand to the brightest angel, is the end and final cause of all creation, the mirror in which the beam of God's brightness comes to rest and so returns to God. Blessed be the Holy One!

God has immeasurable use for each thing that is made, that love and splendour may flow forth like a strong river which has need of a great watercourse and fills alike the deep pools and the little crannies. . . . Blessed be God!

Adapted from C. S. Lewis, *Perelandra* (New York: Macmillan, 1965; original publication, 1944), 214–17, *passim,* with permission of the Estate of C. S. Lewis and The Bodley Head.

Chapter 1

The Reign of God Made Flesh

■

Imagine yourself in a corner of the world of cartoonist Gary Larson ("The Far Side"). Imagine being seated in a living room, surrounded by cola-drinking cows who comment on the world, the weather and the weird ways of humans. Imagine yourself at the Great Dance, where the least leprechaun leaps, lithe and agile as the brightest angel. Imagine yourself gazing into Deep Heaven and seeing there (as Flannery O'Connor once did) "a vast horde of souls . . . whole companies of white-trash, clean for the first time in their lives . . . battalions of freaks and lunatics shouting and clapping and leaping like frogs."[1]

Imagine.

Few of us fully appreciate one of the most original aspects of Jesus' life and work—namely, his conviction that the act of salvation begins with an act of imagination. For Jesus, life is an exclamation, a cry of wonder: the "force that through the green fuse drives the flower"; the "process in the weather of the heart" that turns damp to dry and night

5

to day. The Jesus of the gospels is endlessly attentive to the ways of the world—and to the ways of God in that world. He is portrayed as someone who awakens people to their need for salvation by arousing their hunger for creative imagination. Thus the central theme of Jesus' message—the rule or reign of God—is never portrayed as a theological datum, but always, instead, as an invitation to let fancy take flight. For God's reign, too, is an exclamation: a woman's shout when she finds lost money; a crafty servant's "creative accounting"; a misguided merchant's passion for pearls; an old fool's love for an undeserving son. Jesus recognized that we humans begin to be converted when our creativity is challenged; we begin to be saved when our imaginations are released from their bondage to the preternaturally dull!

Only those can be saved, in Jesus' view, who know—from the raw wound inside their ribs—that they have something they need to be saved from. Helping people discover that *something* was a principal purpose of Jesus' preaching in parables. I will have more to say later about the strategy and significance of these unsettling stories. Here I simply want to emphasize that for Jesus, conversion is a call to creativity; faith frees the heart for fancy; and salvation always starts as a surprise.

Our often unrecognized need to be saved and God's response to that need in provocative, unexpected ways are what Jesus meant by the "reign of God." The notion that God does, can or will act as a ruler (vanquishing enemies, rewarding the righteous and establishing a "new world order") was obviously not invented by Jesus (though use of the phrase "reign of God" was relatively rare among Jews of his day). Two things, however, made Jesus' announcement of the advent of God's reign startlingly new and potentially subversive. First, Jesus' own ministry made it clear that God's "reigning" is neither a place nor a state nor a condition nor (above all!) a concept—but *a divine new way of acting that defies all previous categories of perception and interpretation.* In short, Jesus understood God's reign as an evocative, embodied symbol so richly ambiguous in its reach and range that it subverts every effort to restrict its definition or to control its meanings. Second, Jesus kept insinuating, through parabolic word and deed, that this God who "reigns" is One who acts in a most ungodlike manner. Jesus thus challenged traditional religious views not only about how God behaves, but also about who God is. A few additional comments about these two points are in order.

God's Reign as a Symbol

To say that God's reign is a symbol means that it cannot be reduced to our usual cognitive categories, strategies and structures, for by definition, symbols differ from conceptual experiences. Symbols are not primarily "thought" or "thought about"; they are embodied, performed, enacted. Their roots are buried not merely in our psyches but in our skins: they invade our embraces, encamp among our heartbeats. That is why encountering symbols (in dreams, for instance) can be so unsettling—and so healing—an experience.

In many respects symbols resemble Zen koans, those strange, mind-bending riddles traditionally assigned to disciples seeking enlightenment. "What is the sound of one hand clapping?" The "answer," of course, is everything, or nothing; raucous laughter, or a sharp slap in the face; a loud belch, or a quiet nap. For a koan (like a symbol) cannot be "solved" through the traditional techniques of cognition, conceptualization and logical analysis. The appropriate response is action—or no action—for the point is that we can never reach enlightenment until we abandon our artificially constructed boundaries of thought and theory. The Zen disciple must learn to trust the body's wisdom instinctively and unself-consciously—to sleep when tired;

to eat when hungry. Similarly, symbols invite us to trust actions, not objects—deeds, not concepts. If God's reign is a symbol, then it is an embodied activity that exceeds cognition's capacity to limit its definition, specify its content or determine its uses. The first step in "grasping" a symbol is surrender, not grasping!

The God Who Doesn't Act Like One   Not long ago, a music and drama major at Pomona College in Claremont, California, wrote a 90-minute show called *Come Again?* as his senior project. Its complex and somewhat improbable plot featured Mary, who is pregnant but doesn't want to be, Joe and a bag lady who claims to be God (and tells Joe he's going to be pregnant instead). Preposterous, yes. But perhaps no more so than Jesus' vision of a God who doesn't act like one. For one of the astonishing things about Jesus' understanding of the "reign of God" was its implied redefinition of the Divine. For Jesus, God's act of reigning means that God has become wholly identified with people, has become immediately present to them as unconditional love and acceptance, has become "available" to humanity in heretofore unimaginable (even unclean) ways—as leaven in dough, as Samaritan helping Jew, as mustard in a field of grain, as prodigal parent to problem child.

In a nutshell, God's "reign," for Jesus, is God's own self given over to people. The *reign* of God means the *incarnation* of God. It means that God's lot is now the human one, that henceforth God's power is exercised entirely on behalf of humankind, that God's will is always and only a willing-good. It means, above all, that God's "self" has been emptied, poured out—has become a human-self-with-others. What made Jesus' message so radical, as Thomas Sheehan has noted, was its insistence that the thundering, tree-splitting God who shakes the mountains has now disappeared into humanity—and can be found nowhere else but there.[2] The God of Jesus, quite simply, is a God who refuses to act like one.

The Response of Conversion For Jesus, conversion is the only possible response to this utterly new definition of who God is. God has suddenly arrived in our midst—as babe, as body, as bread, as bounty—and the only thing we can do is start our lives afresh. There can be no holding back. "Follow me—and let the dead bury their own dead!" "If any sue you and take your coat—let them have your cloak as well!" "If you are forced to go a mile with someone—go two." "Blessed are the destitute! Blessed are the reviled! Blessed are the weeping! Blessed are the hungry!" "If you follow me, you carry a cross!" These are not religious principles or sermon ideas; they are, as John Dominic Crossan has aptly put it, "a score to be played and a program to be enacted. . . . In the end, as in the beginning, now as then, there is only the performance."[3]

Persons are performances—and so is God. That is Jesus' shocking conclusion, one that overturns the customary projects of religion: linking finite beings to an infinite God, reconciling imperfect creatures with a perfect Creator. Just as we become persons by enacting ourselves in time and space, within a world and a culture, so God's name and nature become known only as we experience them in our mortal flesh, in the tumultuous textures of our human history. The reign of God becomes the flesh of God, folded in the body of a woman, born under the law, revealed in the world's last age. As Jesuit poet Gerard Manley Hopkins put it,

> Across my foundering deck shone
> A beacon, an eternal beam. Flesh fade, and mortal trash
> Fall to the residuary worm; world's wildfire, leave but ash:
> In a flash, at a trumpet crash,
> I am all at once what Christ is, since he was what I am, and
> This Jack, joke, poor potsherd, patch, matchwood,
>   immortal diamond
> Is immortal diamond.[4]

For Jesus, then, God's presence in and as people cannot happen apart from what the New Testament calls *metanoia,* conversion, a complete about-face. The reign-of-God-made-flesh becomes the demand that we let God's presence happen through lives of justice and charity. Thomas Sheehan has made this point forcefully:

> Although the kingdom [reign] was entirely God's gift . . . the offer of God's presence turned into the challenge to let it happen; the invitation to the kingdom became the demand to live the dawning future—God's reign—in the present moment. Living the future in the present meant doing "violence" to the kingdom (Luke 16:16), not, however, by storming its walls with one's virtues or bribing one's way in with religious observance. The "violence" of living the future in the present was *metanoia,* "repentance." That did not mean self-flagellation for one's sins but "turning oneself around" and wholly changing one's life into an act of justice and mercy toward others. In Jesus' message, the invitation and the response were interdependent. The promised presence of God was the meaning of the demand for justice and charity, and yet only in such acts of mercy did the eschatological future become present.
>
> This mutuality—eschatology as the ground of ethics, and ethics as the realization of eschatology—is what made Jesus' moral demands so radical. . . . Charity fulfills the Law—not because it *makes* God present, but because it *is* [God's] presence.[5]

Forgiveness, the Future's Name   Not only, then, did Jesus redefine God, he redefined time as well. We are used to thinking of time only as linear and chronological, as "before" and "after," as this followed by that. But Jesus' vision—of God as person and performance, of God's reign "made flesh," of God's presence in and as people—shattered the usual chronological categories by which we "keep" time (itself an interesting image!). In their place Jesus proposed a nonchronological understanding of time, one that can no longer be plotted on a linear timetable of "bygones" and "not-yets." Thus, for Jesus the past is not what happened yesterday but the reign of sin and Satan, the awful burden of alienation from God, the weight of all that is impenetrable to God's gift of self.

Similarly the future, in Jesus' view, is not tomorrow but God's reign—the performance (enactment) of God's presence here and now, in lives of justice, compassion and mercy. Conversion means crossing over from past to future—and the line that marks the difference between these two ages is called forgiveness.

It is important, however, not to think of forgiveness as the cancellation of a debt or the erasure of mistakes or the overlooking of sins by a God who's grown weary of keeping records in a little black book. Forgiveness is not the end of a bartering process by which we hold God hostage to our accumulated virtue. Instead, forgiveness means crossing the line—living the future instead of living the past. What is "given" in "for-giveness" is nothing less than God. To be forgiven is to welcome God's arrival in the present moment; it is to experience and embrace God's self-communicating incarnation. So intensely was Jesus gripped by this vision that he let himself be swept up by God's uncontrollable present-future. God's reign, writes Thomas Sheehan, became Jesus' "madness. He celebrated it with anyone who would join him at table, declared everyone free in its name, broke all rules that stood in its way, and finally gave up his life for it."[6] Jesus thus became what he proclaimed: the presence of God among women and men, the reign of God made flesh.

A Place Called Hope

During the 1992 presidential campaign, Bill Clinton often referred to his birthplace (and to his vision for a renewed American society) as "a place called Hope." Hope, of course, is possible only for people who believe that change is needed and obtainable and that change would be beneficial for them. People who perceive change as threatening—or impossible—are rarely hopeful. The momentum for change (and the hope that fuels it) emerges from people in transition, from those who know the *status quo* has got to go. Hope is thus closely connected to conversion; it is, as Emily Dickinson once described it,

> The thing with feathers—
> That perches in the soul—
> And sings the tune without the words—
> And never stops—at all—[7]

The parables of Jesus have everything to do with this process of conversion—with transition, hope and change. As they were shaped and spliced into the New Testament narratives, Jesus' original parables often were edited for catechetical, theological and ethical purposes: to instruct newcomers, to support pet theories, to promote certain behaviors. This reshaping of the Jesus tradition (which writers, theologians, preachers and catechists have continued to do throughout two millennia) was natural and inevitable—but it also meant that much of the original "bite" and impact of Jesus' message was muted, muzzled. Many of the parables were sifted (to lessen their shock), softened (to avoid giving offense), expanded (for use as morality tales) and explained (for use as teaching tools).

A good illustration of this process can be seen in the famous story of the sower (see Mark 4:3b−8, and parallels) and its appended explanation (see Mark 4:13−20). Scripture scholars generally agree that while the parable itself (e.g., Mark 4:3b−8) reflects something Jesus probably said in his ministry, the explanation represents a later—and different—tradition. We are fortunate today to have tools that present in a clear, intelligible fashion the consensus of modern scholarship on Jesus' parables and the ways they have been altered in early Christian literature.[8]

In what follows, I will rely on the best modern critical judgments about Jesus' own parables and about their multiple meanings—there is never only one! I will be especially interested in the way the world of parable subverts traditional religious sensibilities and invites hearers to embrace the work of conversion. I will also show how such conversion is essential to the entire process of Christian initiation stretching from precatechumenate to mystagogy, and especially to participation in the eucharist as the "climax and completion" of the sacraments of initiation.

Bernard Brandon Scott, one of North America's premier parable scholars, has noted that the world projected by Jesus' parables is characterized by several highly original strategies.[9] If we are to understand the unique and radical character of Jesus' message and the way it shaped his table ministry, it will be worth our while to take a closer look at these strategies. For the eucharist is nothing less than the Christian community's ritualized embodiment of Jesus' own parabolic "table manners." Jesus' call to conversion (and his call to come to the table) is rooted in five basic — and rather startling — convictions:

1) Grace (that is, God's own presence, self, life) comes to those who have "hit bottom."

2) God's reign is recognized not by its grandeur but by its *everydayness.*

3) The advent of God's world subverts the world of "business as usual."

4) Faith happens when one finds the courage to surrender to a God who acts in an *ungodlike* manner.

5) In God's paradoxical world, the face of comedy is often tragic.

Let's look at the way Jesus embodies these convictions in parable.

Grace Comes to Those Who Have "Hit Bottom"

Consider the well-known parable of the Good Samaritan. The traveler in the ditch may not have been especially ecstatic about accepting help from a Samaritan — indeed, he may have preferred to wait and take his chances that a good Jewish layman would happen by (since the clergy were of no help). But when you're lying wounded **13** in a ditch your options are severely limited. As Bernard Scott remarks,

> Grace comes to those who cannot resist, *who have no other alternative than to accept it. To enter the parable's World, to get into the ditch, is to be so low that grace is the only alternative.* The point may be so simple as this: only [those] who [need] grace can receive grace.[10]

Hitting bottom is also a feature of many modern stories written in a parabolic mode. One of my favorites is Flannery O'Connor's grisly tale, "A Good Man Is Hard to Find." In it, a rather comically dysfunctional Southern family decides to take a vacation by car. From the beginning, the trip is marred by controversy and bickering. Grandmother (a devout churchgoer and animal lover who secretly brings her pet cat, Pitty Sing, along for the journey) wants to visit relatives in east Tennessee; her son Bailey and his wife and children want to go to Florida. Their quarreling and refusal to compromise takes them on bad back roads where, not surprisingly, all the bumps and jostling spook the cat, which leaps onto Bailey's back, causing him to jerk the steering wheel and send the car careening over a steep embankment. The family finds itself literally in the ditch, when suddenly out of the dark, surrounding woods a "Good Samaritan" appears. But this Samaritan—who calls himself "The Misfit"—is quite a bit more than the family bargained for. An escapee from prison, The Misfit explains to the startled (and increasingly frightened) travelers that he had once been a gospel singer, a soldier and (most ominously) an undertaker—but all that was before he was sent to the penitentiary. To Grandmother, who keeps repeating that they should all pray and trust Jesus, The Misfit retorts,

> Jesus thrown everything off balance. It was the same case with Him as with me except He hadn't committed any crime and they could prove I had committed one because they had the papers on me. Of course . . . they never shown me my papers. . . . I call myself The Misfit . . . because I can't make what all I done wrong fit all I gone through in punishment. . . . Does it

seem right to you, lady, that one is punished a heap and another ain't punished at all?[11]

While Grandmother and The Misfit "talk religion," the rest of the family is escorted by the latter's companions into the woods. Screams and shots are heard, and Grandmother realizes with growing horror that her son, daughter-in-law and grandchildren are being brutally, systematically executed. The ditch where the wrecked automobile lies is fast becoming a grave. Still the surreal conversation between Grandmother and The Misfit continues:

> "Jesus was the only One that ever raised the dead." The Misfit continued, "and He shouldn't have done it. He thrown everything off balance. If He did what He said, then it's nothing for you to do but throw away everything and follow Him, and if He didn't, then it's nothing for you to do but enjoy the few minutes you got left the best way you can—by killing somebody or burning down his house or doing some other meanness to him. No pleasure but meanness," he said and his voice had become almost a snarl.[12]

At that moment Grandmother hits absolute bottom. She has no alternative but to reach out to the "source of grace" that stands brandishing a gun in front of her. "'Why, you're one of my babies,' she cries, 'you're one of my own children!'" Then she lifts an arm to touch The Misfit on the shoulder. He springs back "as if a snake had bitten him," and pumps three bullets into the old woman's chest. Then he calmly takes off his glasses and begins cleaning them on his shirtsleeve.

Horrifying as it is, "A Good Man is Hard to Find" represents a kind of modern version of the biblical story. Just as Jesus' parable reverses his hearer's expectations (in traditional storytelling, the third person coming down the road should have been a helpful Jewish layperson), so O'Connor's story subverts modern expectations (Good Samaritans should help, not hinder; give life, not take it away). Both biblical parable and modern story confront us with situations where we have no alternative but to accept the proffered help—even when it isn't the kind of help we want or expect or approve of. For Grandmother, grace comes, literally, as a speeding bullet. And in his twisted way, The Misfit recognizes this. "She would of been a good woman," he concludes at the story's end, "if it had been somebody there to shoot her every minute of her life." Coldly brutal? Yes. Pathological? Yes. But recall Jesus' acerbic one-liner, "Leave the dead to bury their own dead!"

God's Reign Is Recognized by Its Everydayness

In Jesus' parables, it is not religious doctrine or insight that serves as a lens to interpret the "everyday," but the opposite. Everyday experience is the paradigm for religious experience. Parables do not intend to illustrate a theological point or shore up a religious symbol. On the contrary, it is their purpose to question theological assumptions, to challenge ingrained habits of denial, to subvert customary claims that religious ideals inspire our choices and motives. As Bernard Scott notes, "Jesus' images are natural, secular images. . . . The key to their openness is within them."[13] Reality, for Jesus, is not divided into "sacred vs. secular," "in vs. out," "light vs. darkness," or "us vs. them." Rejecting such commonly and widely held dualisms, Jesus offers a vision of God-with-humanity in which the routines of daily life *are* (not "are made" or "are interpreted as") revelatory experiences of the Divine.

Thomas Sheehan makes a similar point when he notes that Jesus' vision of God's reign—of living the present-future and crossing the line called forgiveness—means maintaining "the *undecidability* of what is human and what is divine."[14] This is, of course, a prime characteristic of everyday life, with its messy ambiguity, its mixed messages, its combined grandeur and tawdriness. Parables remind us not to be too hasty in calling this "virtue" or that "vice."

Consider this brief, pungent parable, which virtually all scholars claim comes directly from Jesus:

> The kingdom of heaven is like leaven which a woman took and hid in three measures of flour, till it was all leavened. (Matthew 13:33b)

Notice, first, that the images are thoroughly domestic, ordinary and everyday—far removed from the rarified religious atmosphere of temple, cult, priesthood or rabbinate. Second, note that the story's three major motifs—leaven, a woman and hiding—are all problematic, given the usual religious opinions of Jesus' day. The acceptable view would have portrayed God's reign as unleavened (hence, pure and undefiled), as represented by males, and as open (revealed, not hidden). Both cultural and religious assumptions are challenged by this short story.

Virtually all ancient Mediterranean cultures used "leaven" as a metaphor for spreading corruption (much like our "one bad apple")—just as they used women as symbols for uncleanness and impurity. Yet here comes Jesus, announcing that God's reign is both leavenlike and womanlike! Moreover, in typical Jewish family life (see Jeremiah 7:18), kneading dough is appropriate work for women—yet this story says the woman *hid the leaven* (a stealthy, secretive deed).

The real kicker comes in the story's last phrase: "till it was *all* leavened [*all* corrupted]"! Modern yeast is domesticated; in the ancient world, it had to be made from scratch by storing a piece of bread in a dark, dank place until it began to rot, decay and mold. The end of the leavening process was not baked bread with its fragrant odor and golden crust, but rising dough with its fermented, yeasty, rotting scent. Of course! But what a shocking, unsavory image for the reign of God! The very idea that this everyday world—a *woman's* world—could actually *be* the experience of God's reign was preposterous. How, in the name of all that is holy, could the God who reigns be revealed by this everyday world—where a sneaky woman hides smelly leaven until everything rots? Scandalous! As John Dominic Crossan has said, commenting on this parable, "a woman hiding leaven in her dough: It's there, it's natural, it's necessary, but society has a problem with it."[15]

Observe, then, that in this tiny story the everyday serves as a paradigm for religious experience—not vice versa. It is precisely the woman's act of hiding leaven "until it all rots" (so Jesus insists) that reveals God at work in the world. Even today we find this a very difficult parable to accept. How can something "rotten" be "good"? How can women's work reveal "the God of Abraham, Isaac and Jacob" (we conveniently overlook "the God of Sarah, Rebecca and Rachel")? Jesus' "innocent" little tale is "diaphoric"—it tells a story by means of *dissimilarity,* disjunction; it exposes something radically new by putting together things never before joined. The parable thus assaults some of our most cherished notions about what is ethical, good and holy, and about where and how God's reign erupts in human life. Bernard Scott has sharply summarized this parable's challenge:

> The kingdom (the holy and good) is pictured in terms of an epiphany of corruption. How radical is the parable's intention? Does it mean to state that good is evil in an ethics of absurdity? Or is its function to subvert a hearer's ready dependency on the rules of the sacred, the predictability of what is good, and warn that instead the expected evil that corrupts may indeed turn out to be the kingdom. . . .
>
> Such a discourse is corroborated by Jesus' association with the outcast. . . . The kingdom is present among the marginal. . . . In the end, the parable, because it is diaphor, can have no closure, because it seeks to join what cannot be joined. The parable calls into question ready attempts to predict on the basis of our knowledge of the holy and good where the kingdom is active. Instead it insists on the kingdom's freedom to appear under its own guise, even if it be the guise of corruption.[16]

The everyday. The undecidability of what is human and what is divine within the turbulent vortex of history. Perhaps parable confronts us once more with the wisdom of Philo, the Jewish scholar of Alexandria:

> When the righteous search for the nature of all things, they make their own marvelous discovery: That *all is God's grace.* . . .

Everything in the world—even the very world itself—manifests the blessings and generosity of God.[17]

The Parable's World Challenges the Hearer's World The point just concluded stressed the crucial connection between parables and everyday experience. But it is important to add that parables do not simply refer back to everydayness; they rearrange it, render it different or even bizarre. Parables burlesque everyday order and experience, and thereby call it into question. Common stereotypes (Samaritan = wicked) are rejected; strangely inappropriate images (kingdom = leaven) are invoked. Suddenly the familiar world looks vastly unfamiliar; the precarious boundary between reality and illusion blurs. One is forced to decide between the hearer's world (business as usual) and the parable's world (the reign of God enfleshed in a woman's act of hiding leaven). Deciding to risk everything in order to embrace the parable is the first step toward *metanoia,* conversion. It is thus also the first step in coming to the Lord's table.

Perhaps no theologian has understood this point as keenly as Flannery O'Connor (though she would have hated being called a theologian, a group for whom—apart from Aquinas—she had little time or patience!). Her story "Revelation" shows us worlds in conflict. The world of everyday virtue, goodness and common sense is represented by jovial, loquacious Ruby Turpin, a devout, church-going woman who is utterly oblivious to her racism, dishonesty and deep prejudices. The disruptive, parabolic world is represented by Mary Grace, an acne-scarred student at Wellesley who is vacationing in her native Georgia. The two meet in a doctor's waiting room one sultry summer afternoon. As gospel hymns float softly over the air from a radio in the corner, Ruby reflects on her "religious principles:"

> To help anybody out that needed it was her philosophy of life. She never spared herself when she found somebody in need,

19

whether they were white or black, trash or decent. And of all she had to be thankful for, she was most thankful that this was so. If Jesus had said, "You can be high society and have all the money you want and be thin and svelte-like, but you can't be a good woman with it," she would have had to say, "Well don't make me that then. Make me a good woman and it don't matter what else, how fat or how ugly or how poor!" Her heart rose. He had not made her a nigger or white-trash or ugly! He had made her herself and given her a little of everything. Jesus, thank you! she said. Thank you thank you thank you![18]

All the while that Ruby is silently thanking Jesus, Mary Grace is glowering at her from behind a huge book she is reading. As Ruby's heart lifts in gratitude, Mary Grace's gorge rises in rage. At last, neither woman can contain herself. Inspired by the gospel tunes and by her inborn feeling of superiority, Ruby blurts out,

When I think who all I could have been besides myself and what all I got, a little of everything, and a good disposition besides, I just feel like shouting, "Thank you, Jesus, for making everything the way it is!" It could have been different! . . . "Oh thank you Jesus, Jesus, thank you."[19]

At that exact moment, Mary Grace hurls her book and herself at Ruby, knocking her senseless to the floor. Then, slowly,

Mrs. Turpin's head cleared and her power of motion returned. She leaned forward until she was looking directly into [Mary Grace's] fierce brilliant eyes. *There was no doubt in her mind that the girl did know her, knew her in some intense and personal way, beyond time and place and condition.* "What you got to say to me?" [Ruby] asked hoarsely and held her breath, waiting, *as for a revelation.*

The girl raised her head. Her gaze locked with Mrs. Turpin's. "Go back to hell where you came from, you old wart hog," she whispered. Her voice was low but clear. Her eyes burned for a moment as if she saw with pleasure that her message had struck its target.

Mrs. Turpin sank back in her chair.[20]

Here, as always, the parable's world burlesques the respectable, virtuous, grateful, good-humored world of the everyday. Grace comes enfleshed as a scarred, psychotically disturbed young woman who, for all her limits, sees clearly through Mrs. Turpin's illusory world of self-righteous gratitude and religiosity. Ruby's first reaction to the revelation is not, of course, acceptance of its truth. Rather she responds with rage and defensiveness. To God, she complains bitterly,

> "Why me? . . . It's no trash around here, black or white, that I haven't given to. And break my back to the bone every day working. And do for the church. . . .
>
> "If you like trash better, go get yourself some trash. . . .
>
> "Go on . . . call me a hog! Call me a hog again. From hell. Call me a wart hog from hell. Put that bottom rail on top. There'll still be a top and bottom!"
>
> A final surge of fury shook her and she roared, "Who do you think you are?"[21]

Which is exactly the point. Parable subverts the everyday world of both "secular reality" and "religious meaning," exposing them as self-serving and duplicitous. It requires a radical redefinition of God, one that will not connive with our sexist, racist, exclusivist versions of human society. By story's end, the parabolic strategy has swept away Ruby's defensiveness and opened her eyes to the first light of conversion:

> She raised her hands . . . in a gesture hieratic and profound. A visionary light settled in her eyes. She saw . . . a vast horde of souls . . . rumbling toward heaven . . . bands of black niggers in white robes, and battalions of freaks and lunatics shouting and clapping and leaping like frogs. *And bringing up the end of the procession was a tribe of people whom she recognized at once as those who, like herself . . . had always had a little of everything and the God-given wit to use it right. . . . She could see by their shocked and altered faces that even their virtues were being burned away. . . .* In a moment the vision faded but she remained where she was, immobile.
>
> At length she . . . made her slow way on the darkening path to the house. In the woods around her the invisible cricket choruses had struck up, but what she heard were the voices of the souls climbing upward into the starry field and shouting hallelujah.[22]

Faith Consists of Finding the Courage to Trust the World Depicted by the Parable As the story "Revelation" shows so powerfully, faith begins only when the hearer surrenders the illusory world of the quotidian, and steps into the "brave new world" of parable. This step is often humiliating, painful and frightening. If I'm lying wounded in a ditch, what assurance do I have that the Samaritan intends to help rather than murder? If I've just been decked by a vicious young student from Wellesley, what assurance do I have that her message comes from God? Faith arises when we begin trusting the parable's version of reality even when it fails to provide comforting assurances that "all will be well." Bernard Scott has summed it up succinctly: "The contrary of faith is ideology."[23] Ideology, as described by Mike Cormack,

> can be seen as a complex process by which our experience of the world is structured. Its source lies in our own socio-economic origins. It functions to reproduce that originating condition. The patterns of power in society are repeated in ideology, with the ideology of the powerful being the dominating form of understanding in any society. An ideology is not . . . a simple, undifferentiated structure, but a complex of overlapping and sometimes contradictory elements articulated together.[24]

In short, ideological structures are well known, predictable, predetermined. There are no surprises. The world is clearly and categorically divided (haves/have nots; superior/inferior; powerful/powerless; clean/unclean; trash/decent; etc.). To conform to ideological "reality" is to respect and preserve those categories at all costs—even if they conflict with evidence gleaned from our experience of the world. The decisive thing about ideologies is that they resolutely maintain their illusion of "truthfulness" in the face of massive evidence to the contrary.

Parables challenge such predetermined predictability, inviting hearers to make judgment for themselves on the basis of what they see and hear. (How often in the gospels Jesus remarks, "You have ears—use them! You have eyes—

open them!") Recall the story of the feast (Matthew 22:2–13; Luke 14:16b–24).[25] It's the famous (and humiliating) situation of sending RSVP invitations to a dinner party—and receiving "no's" from all the invitees. The social ambiance of the story is instructive. Clearly the host is wealthy, for in the ancient world only the affluent could afford the double system of invitation implied by the narrative (Matthew 22:16b–17). The courtesy reminder (second invitation), moreover, suggests that the guests had already accepted the first invitation. So the message is sharply pointed: Through a series of late and lame excuses, the host is being deliberately insulted, rejected and shamed. Given the code of honor and shame governing social behavior in ancient Mediterranean cultures, we should expect the host to match insult for insult ("You snub me and I'll snub you!" "I won't get mad, I'll get even!"). And in fact, the host does respond in the expected manner, angrily snubbing the original invitees by throwing the feast open to a motley crowd of misfits—indeed, to anyone who can be pulled in off the streets (see Luke 14:21–23).

The kicker, of course, is that while such revenge is sweet, it does nothing to restore the host's loss of face and honor. Just as his social prestige would have been enhanced by those originally invited (obviously people of means and standing), so now he is trapped by his own retaliatory gambit. His house is full of nobodies—social outcasts, homeless street people—exactly the kinds of guests who cannot give him the honor he craves. Chagrin follows insult. Doing the socially correct thing (a snub for a snub) brings about even greater loss of face. The story cleverly exposes the Achilles' heel of the "shame-and-honor" system of social mores. It challenges the predictable world of social ideology (which demands getting even) by showing how such a system succeeds in destroying the honor of those who use it!

Once more the familiar parabolic strategy can be detected: A secular situation serves as paradigm for religious experience. Just as the meal in the story has ultimate social significance for the host (his honor and prestige depend on it), so the feast (Jesus implies) signals matters of ultimate import: entry into God's reign, salvation. Naturally, one expects such matters to be marked by a degree of grandeur and solemnity, decorum and weightiness. In the context of Jewish messianic hopes, the banquet should be a joyful occasion that restores honor to those who have suffered for their fidelity to God. The feast of God's reign should (one thus assumes) be an impressive affair, unfolding with a certain style, grace and elegance. One imagines tables draped in damask, Royal Doulton china and a string ensemble playing Haydn quartets. But not so. The guests are the uninvited, the miserable, the smelly; the palsied schizophrenic, the mumbling borderline psychotic, the heroin addict who lives in a cardboard box under a thundering overpass. As Bernard Scott has noted,

> The parable reverses and subverts the system of honor. The man who gives a banquet loses his honor and joins the shameless poor. An audience expects the messianic banquet to signal that those who have suffered at the hands of Israel's enemies will be restored to honor by the power of God. Here the opposite happens. Paradoxically, in the Jesus parable the guest without the wedding garment would have remained.[26]

This is hardly the predictable world of social and religious rewards we have been reared to expect. What is depicted by the parable is not our familiar, if often informal, system of rewards and punishments, debits and credits, favors and paybacks ("You owe me one"). On the contrary, the parable questions the criteria we routinely employ to determine divisions between virtue and vice, sacred and secular, divine deeds versus the merely human. It raises the discomfiting possibility that perhaps—just perhaps—we really do not know what's best for us, in spite of our devout plans and good intentions.

Once again, Flannery O'Connor can guide us through

the parabolic thickets of virtue gone awry. In her story

"The Lame Shall Enter First," we encounter a classic example of someone whose good intentions mask an inner emptiness. Sheppard is a widower puzzled and annoyed by his ten-year-old son, Norton, who continues to mourn his mother's death more than a year after the fact. Emotionally estranged from his child, whose prolonged grief strikes him as selfish, Sheppard turns outward to worthy liberal causes. On weekends, he works without wages as a counselor at the local reformatory, where he meets Rufus Johnson, an abused African American teenager whose mother is in a state prison. Rufus "was raised by his grandfather in a shack without water or electricity and the old man beat him every day."[27]

Sheppard decides to devote his energies to rehabilitating the boy, who is—not surprisingly—undernourished, emotionally maimed, and severely crippled by a clubfoot. Norton is dismayed to discover that his father plans to adopt Rufus and has given him a key to their house. Predictably, the two boys do not get along, but Sheppard blithely maintains that their conflict is temporary and will vanish once Norton recovers from his mournful selfishness. Meanwhile, Rufus sorely tests Sheppard's patience and liberal goodwill—skulking about, talking mean, bullying Norton, vandalizing homes in the neighborhood, running away.

The whole situation comes to a head when Rufus is picked up by the police and brought back to Sheppard's home. An ugly confrontation follows, in which the boy hints that Sheppard has made immoral suggestions to him. Asked by a reporter just what these suggestions were, Rufus replies,

"He's a dirty atheist. . . . He said there wasn't no hell. . . ."

"Wait," Sheppard said. . . . "Tell the truth, Rufus. . . . You don't want to perpetrate this lie. You're not evil, you're mortally confused. You don't have to make up for that foot, you don't have to . . ."

Johnson hurled himself forward. "Listen at him!" he screamed. "I lie and steal because I'm good at it! My foot don't have a thing to do with it! The lame shall enter first! The halt'll be gathered together. When I get ready to be saved, Jesus'll save me, not that lying stinking atheist.[28]

In typical O'Connor fashion, this moment of grinding, angry confrontation becomes the terrible instant of revelation and grace. Stung cruelly by Rufus's accusations, Sheppard's eyes are finally opened. "I did more for him than I did for my own child," he admits, with crushing candor. Then the abyss opens:

> His heart constricted with a repulsion for himself so clear and intense that he gasped for breath. *He had stuffed his own emptiness with good works like a glutton. He had ignored his own child to feed his vision of himself.* He saw the clear-eyed Devil, the sounder of hearts, leering at him from the eyes of Johnson. His image of himself shrivelled until everything was black before him. He sat there paralyzed, aghast.[29]

At last, Sheppard understands that his own will and emotions have been paralyzed, that the selfishness of which he accused Norton was really his own:

> A rush of agonizing love for the child rushed over him like a transfusion of life. The little boy's face appeared to him transformed; the image of his salvation; all light. He groaned with joy. . . . He jumped up and ran to his room, to tell him that he loved him, that he would never fail him again.[30]

But Norton is not in his bed. Sheppard races frantically through the house, searching—and then remembers that Norton often spent hours alone in the attic, where he gazed at the sky through a telescope, hoping to find his mother among the stars. Up the stairs Sheppard flies, only to reel back when he reaches the top. The tripod that held the telescope in place had fallen to the floor, and "A few feet over it, the child hung in the jungle of shadows, just below the beam from which he had launched his flight into space."[31]

This time, grace comes not as a speeding bullet through the chest (as in "A Good Man is Hard to Find"), or a book hurled through the air (as in "Revelation"), but as a child swinging in the jumbled shadows of an attic. Just as in the parable of the great feast, the host finds himself scorned and dishonored, at table with outcasts, so in this story a father finds himself shamed and destroyed by "good intentions." The parables suggest—shockingly—that this is what God's reign is like! Trusting the world of the parable is, then, something quite different from a Pollyannaish confidence in bright skies and butterflies. It means trusting when there is absolutely no rational reason to trust. It means surrendering when to do so looks like certain death. How do you know the Samaritan won't kill you? You don't. You first have to trust, to take the risk of letting him pull you from the ditch. Only then can the stranger be recognized as a savior.

In Parable, Comedy's Face Is Tragic In classical drama, comedy does not necessarily provoke romping laughter; it is, rather, a plot describing a protagonist's progress toward *well-being*. Similarly, tragedy is a plot showing a protagonist's inexorable movement toward unhappiness or *catastrophe*. As Dan Via has summarized it,

> In comedy we have an upward movement toward well-being and the inclusion of the protagonist in a new or renewed society, while in tragedy we have a plot falling toward catastrophe and the isolation of the protagonist from society.[32]

The parable of the prodigal son seems "comic" in that it reveals "an upward movement from destitution and despair to physical well-being and personal reconciliation in a renewed society."[33] By contrast, the great feast seems tragic because the protagonist (the host) moves toward disappointment and isolation from the (presumably joyful) world of respectable society.

In the context of Jesus' parables, however, such neat summaries of plot structure and character development are shaken up. Comic and tragic elements do indeed abound in the parables, but their reach and relations are significantly altered. For one thing, parabolic comedy is not only an ascent toward happiness and inclusion, it is also, as Robert Funk has observed, a movement from illusion to reality, "from a society bound by law, custom, tradition, the old guard to a society given over to the avant-garde, youth, and freedom."[34] To put it another way, illusion is the literal, the fixed, the predictable, the definable, the status quo; comedy's job is to reveal reality by subverting all that.

Jesus' parables, therefore, consistently lampoon the illusory world of cliques and clichés. This is one of the things that differentiated Jesus' view of God's advent from that of his cousin John. Both Jesus and John thought *something* was coming—but who or what? Peering into the future, John saw a world afire, blazing with apocalyptic trauma and wrathful judgment (see Matthew 3:1–12). Peering into the present, Jesus saw God's joyful, buoyant arrival—an unexpected blossoming of grace that overturns the status quo and ridicules the humorless righteousness of self-appointed "saints." Summarizing the contrasts between these two very different views, Robert Funk has written:

> The difference between the apocalypse of John and the apocalyptic language of Jesus is the comic character of the latter. . . . Jesus indulges in the comic distortion of mundane reality as the means of evoking a vision of the approaching new world. The kingdom Jesus anticipates is the present world stood on its head. John is deadly serious and consequently tiring. Jesus is funny and therefore interesting. . . .
>
> The comic apocalypse . . . offers itself only for what it is, the ecstatic vision of a world waiting to be born. It requires a perpetual standing-out (*ek-stasis*) into the future. Just as it debunks the going order, it extends its vision with comic relief: He who looks and waits for that world deserves to be punished for blasphemy, is insane, or is to be put down as a fool and left to his own devices! [35]

There is, then, an essentially comic aspect to Jesus' parables, aphorisms and one-liners. Imagine the host at the great feast—bathed and perfumed with the best gels and lotions, dressed to the nines in an Armani outfit—reduced to sharing a divan at dinner with a stinking crowd of yahoos dragged in off the streets. The reign of God is like this? Imagine a woman squandering precious fuel and light looking for a coin that didn't amount to much in the first place—then squandering even more precious resources on a party for her friends! The reign of God is like that?

Through such stories, Jesus destabilized the status quo, challenged religious and moral clichés, questioned the abstract fixations of dogma, and rearranged the everydayness of the world. Implicit in such a strategy is that *both the storyteller and the hearers must risk tragedy in order to gain the comic ending.* Looming in the corner of every comic parable is the shadow of the cross. The wounded traveler risks choosing between the ditch (slow, certain death) and the Samaritan (another robber? a murderer? a savior?). The affluent host risks irreversible loss of face (if he does nothing to repay snub for snub) or further shame and dishonor (dinner with a bunch of stinking fools). What advice would you give them? Whose side are you on? (You must risk, too.) As Stanley Hopper once wrote, "Fixation crucifies. The Cross occurs whenever Primordial Being [Being that by its very nature can never be controlled or fixed] is unheard, elided, or refused."[36] The storyteller (Jesus) risks the cross because his words may be robbed of their creative ambiguity and reduced to literal meaning—and because his truth may be buried under "an avalanche of moralizing commentary."[37] Hearers risk the cross because the parable confronts them with choices whose terms they neither create nor control. To achieve comic ending, one must risk increasing tragedy:

> It is customary to identify the cross as the illusion-dispelling factor in the Christian gospel. The cross seems solidly real. But of course it holds a dead man. The cross has the same realism as tragedy: submission to inexorable fate. It is hardly ever noticed that the inert figure on the cross has a smile on his lips: The world into which he entered . . . has made a mockery of fate because anchored in something transcending the demonic powers. The recognition scenes in the parables are humorous

because they involve a reversal of the substantial, comfortable, patent nexus of things and relations that constitutes the received world. We are obliged to laugh when the somber judge trips on his robe and knocks the bailiff across the clerk's lap. . . . Such reversals of the dignity of law and the moral earnestness of religion are not funny, of course, to the Pharisees, whose vocation it is to maintain the illusion.[38]

The parables, then, invite conversion because they invite risking the cross for the sake of the comic. It must be remembered that parables—like persons, like God—are performances, not "stories about" but "enactments of." The everyday is not "about" our relation with God, it is that relation. The tragicomic is not "about" God's reign, it is that reign. Bottoming out is not "about" powerlessness and surrender, it is powerlessness and surrender. Trusting the unknown and unpredictable is not "about" faith, it is faith.

In the life and ministry of Jesus, risk and reward, cross and comedy, are focused above all in the enacted parable of the table. There, the chief Diner becomes dinner, the Deliverer becomes a debtor, the Host becomes a hostess (doing "women's work") and the "proper rules of social rank" are disrupted by scandalous egalitarianism. We must turn to the table, then, if we are to understand where the parabolic path of conversion ultimately leads.

Table of Dreams

In his classic study, *Rediscovering the Teaching of Jesus,* Norman Perrin pointed out that Jesus' table-companionship with "tax collectors and sinners" was not a "proclamation in words . . . but an acted parable."[39] It was, Perrin went on to observe, "the aspect of Jesus' ministry which must have been most meaningful to his followers and most offensive to his critics." In chapter two I will have more to say about the radical nature of Jesus' table practices. For the moment, however, I want to concentrate on Perrin's point that the table is a parable (like Jesus' life and preaching, like the cross).

Table Talk   It is an anthropological and sociological truism that to talk of table is to speak of social structures and relationships. This became true, for at least some members of our species, when we moved from subsistence economies (where hunting and gathering food occupied most of the available time, skill and resources) to more stable, affluent economies (where food is abundant and accessible). (One notes, however, that in a world where much hunger exists—largely because of inequitable systems of distribution—many peoples are still unable to move beyond a subsistence economy.) Such a cultural and economic transition permitted the fortunate among us to develop elaborate notions both about what foods signify and about the social contexts in which they are shared. Our attention shifted away from preoccupations about the *quantity* of food (always central where scarcity is the rule) to thoughts about its *preparation* (the culinary arts), its *presentation* (its visual impact on diners), and its *consumption* (the refined rules of etiquette that govern amounts and kinds of food, the sequence of serving and who eats what with whom).

In short, as our species has evolved so has its understanding of food and dining. While we are not the only animals who use nutrition as a way to differentiate between individuals and groups, we may very well be the only ones who "in order to exhibit [their] social position, will deliberately forego food which is wholesome but associated with low social status."[40] In a word, we humans habitually link food to prestige.

> Some dishes are meant to be eaten within the family circle; others are openly offered to guests. Some foods reflect financial stress, others symbolize affluence. [Men and women] can eat more than [they] require to satisfy [their] hunger, simply to impress other people. The importance of prestige food is not a question of how much pleasure is derived from its consumption, but of how much social recognition it confers.[41]

Indeed, in some ancient Mediterranean cultures, it appears to have been both custom and good taste for hosts to announce what the banquet had cost and then to give each guest the sum spent on the meal. Recall again Jesus' parable of the great feast. One can see just how much prestige was at stake when the wealthy decided to entertain their friends at dinner! At the same time one can understand how humiliating it would be to lose the opportunity of making a big impression. After all, ostentatious wealth may intimidate the poor, the maimed and the blind, but it won't necessarily impress them. And besides, street people have no wealthy cronies with whom they can gossip about how fabulous and lavish the host's dinner was!

Closely linked to the equation "food equals prestige" is the idea that "food equals competition for status and superiority." One of the best examples of this phenomenon was the ceremonial feast (known as *potlatch)* held by Indian tribes of the North American Pacific coast. During potlatch, valued gifts (e.g., food and blankets) are exchanged and property publicly destroyed in a competitive display of wealth. Guests were expected to return the invitation by spreading a feast where an even greater supply of riches could be exchanged or destroyed. Failure to reciprocate meant that one publicly acknowledged inferiority (lower social status and prestige).

But prestige and competition are not the only things at stake when people assemble to dine. In traditional societies (which ours is not!) membership, belonging, is based on a common sharing of staple foods and food prohibitions. (From this angle, the petition in the Lord's Prayer—"Give us this day our daily bread"—may actually be a petition for inclusion, for belonging and membership in the tribe that prays for the advent of God's reign.) In other words, people are socially grouped and culturally typed by their food habits. "Tell me what you eat," said the famous French epicure Anthelme Brillat-Savarin, "and I'll tell you what [and who!] you are." For this reason, the most prestigious food eaten by a people is not necessarily the rarest, the most costly or the most exotic. On the contrary, it is above all the daily diet, the daily bread, which "was consumed by the ancestors and . . . granted by the supernatural powers," which confers membership and status within a culture. (To understand this point completely, think for a moment of the privileged relation between Italians and pasta.) This may also explain two other regular features of social life: the use of *ordinary* (staple, daily) food in religious rituals, and "food xenophobia" (one group's refusal to consider another "human" because of the food they eat). Food, diet and dining thus become a basis for both belonging and ostracism. To the French, Italians are "spaghetti eaters" (hence, by implication, inferior); to the Italians, the French are "frog eaters" (hence, by definition, repulsive).

Lee Edward Klosinski has summarized these points well in his 1988 doctoral dissertation on "The Meals in Mark":

> The chief insight gleaned from the anthropology of food is that food has the capacity both to serve as the object of human transactions and to symbolize human interaction, relationships and relatedness. Giving and receiving food creates obligations. It involves the creation of matrices of reciprocity and mutuality. It defines relationships and the contours of group boundaries.[42]

In Greco-Roman antiquity (the dominant social world of Jesus' time), table-companionship was thus central to the self-definition and common activity of a group, giving concrete expression to its identity, its criteria for membership, and its ways of achieving social recognition, status and power.[43]

Parable, Table, Cross   We return, then, to the theme outlined at the outset of this section: Jesus' table ministry as acted parable. We have already noted that a premier aspect of Jesus' preaching strategy was to use parable as a means of provoking surprise and conflict in the hearer, thus opening the way to conversion, to a fundamental change of life and attitude. Parables, as we have seen, characteristically subvert expectations, challenge customary convictions and reverse routine roles, rules and reactions. It is probable, moreover, that Jesus told many of these parables when surrounded by disciples, friends and strangers at table.[44] It is not surprising, then, that the table became such a central parabolic focus of Jesus' ministry and social life. Nor is it surprising that Christians early on saw crucial connections between parable, table and cross.

Unfortunately, the link between cross and table is often misunderstood. Many Christians assume that their linkage results from parallel patterns of destruction and death, surrender and sacrifice: The cross is the place where Jesus' bodily life was seized by death; the table ritually renews or reenacts this sacrifice of Jesus' body in an unbloody manner through the offering and consumption of bread and wine. A number of serious problems, both historical and theological, attend such a view, but suffice it to note here that it fails to acknowledge that both cross and table are consummate acts of Jesus' *life*. Certainly the cross culminated in Jesus' dying, but one must not forget that his death—like our own—was a human act. Indeed, its primary significance, then and now, is just this: that in dying on the cross Jesus acted as all humans—as all persons endowed with freedom and spiritual power—do. As Karl Rahner once observed, human death is more than a biological event or necessity:

> It is on deeper grounds than merely biological ones that human nature inherently and inexorably tends towards death as its inevitable goal. The deepest and most ultimate reason for the . . . orientation to death . . . is the freedom of the spirit. It is this . . . that makes [us] mortal.
>
> Freedom is not the power constantly to change one's course of action, but rather the power to decide that which is to be final and definitive in one's life, that which cannot be superseded or replaced, the power to bring into being from one's own resources that which must be, and must not pass away, the summons to a decision that is irrevocable.[45]

Freedom without finality, freedom without a resting place—without decisiveness—is not free at all; rather, it is a futile and frustrating circle of repetition, where decisions lead nowhere because they are always being revised. *Human freedom*, by contrast, is decisive, personal, spiritual—and ultimately irrevocable. It is not something we have, it is something we *are*. Because we are personal freedom, because it is within our innermost nature to form ourselves by our own free acts, because as embodied spirit we can definitively shape our lives as a whole and decide what our "end" is to be, we are able to "perform" our death as a quintessentially human act that brings our nature to completion, beyond all possibility of revision. (This is the case whether our death is a result of slow, deliberate, natural processes or is sudden, tragic and unexpected.) As a free human decision, our death—and its meaning, its significance—endures forever. It completes us, raises us above the continuous and inconclusive flow of time. In a word, death is human freedom come to full maturity. It is "the breaking in of finality upon mere transience"[46]—in much the way that God's reign is the definitive, plenary arrival of divine presence and power in human hearts and history. Rahner expressed this point with great beauty and poignancy:

> The ultimate act of freedom, in which [we] decide [our] own fate totally and irrevocably, is the act in which [we] either *willingly accept or definitively rebel* against [our] own utter impotence, in which [we are] utterly subject to the control of a mystery which cannot be expressed—that mystery which we call God. In death [we humans] are totally withdrawn from [ourselves]. Every power, down to the last vestige of possibility, of autonomously controlling [our] own destiny is taken away from [us]. Thus the exercise of [our] freedom . . . is summed up at this point in one single decision: whether [we] yield everything up or whether everything is taken from [us] by force, whether [we] respond to this radical deprivation of all power by uttering [our] assent in faith and hope to the nameless mystery which we call God, or whether even at this point [we] seek to cling . . . to [our] own autonomy, protest against this fall into helplessness, and, because of our disbelief, suppose that [we are]

> falling into the abyss of nothingness when in reality we are
> falling into the unfathomable depths of God.[47]

We can begin to understand, then, why death is the most painfully ambiguous—and the most decisive—of all our lived experiences. Death is the liveliest, most human act of all—a blessed consummation (the fulfillment of all our free, personal activity) *and* a convulsive catastrophe (a violation of our wills and bodies; an intrusive, shattering destruction). Death is both something we *do* and something we *suffer*. As deed, death is a voluntary human creation—the ongoing work of art that defines a life, a recurrent and essential part of living. Our mistake, however, is to assume that it appears only at the end of life. We forget (or deny) that our death is already and always happening each time we exercise our freedom as spiritual beings. (Recall the personified figure of Death in Ingmar Bergman's moving film, *The Seventh Seal*. Each time the disillusioned knight reaches a decisive crossroads in his life, Death makes his presence known as partner in a chess game. The most chilling—and revelatory—moment occurs when the knight kneels to lay his life before the Lord and to confess his sins, only to discover that the confessor on the other side of the curtained grill is Death!)

Quite literally, our death is being enacted daily, throughout life, with each act of personal freedom whereby we surrender to—or rebel against—the nameless Mystery of God. The Christian call to embrace the cross as Jesus did is not some pathological invitation to inflict torture or injury, but a call to surrender ever more of one's life to God; to abandon every illusory project of control and self-justification; to allow oneself, in loving, trusting faith, to be taken over by Another. When we die—daily or "at the end"—we are confronted with a choice between surrender or solipsism, openness or closure, acceptance or rebellion, faith or despair, the death of Christ or the death of Adam. We inch our way toward that choice each moment of our lives until, at last, we enter that state of supreme solitude (we call it "dying") where a final decision is demanded of us. Will we reject death, in rage and remorse, as a cruel dying of the light—or will we receive it as our own salvation?

For the Christian, of course, this fateful moment has been radically decided at baptismal initiation. In Paul's classic formula,

> We who were baptized into Christ Jesus were baptized into his death. We were buried with him through baptism into death, so that, just as Christ was raised from the dead by the glory of the Father, we too might live in newness of life (Romans 6:3–4).

Our death has already been rehearsed, and its outcome— a life of eternal goodness lived in God's presence—has been decided. But there is something more to mention here. More often than not we think of Jesus' death as the mournful antithesis of his resurrection, with Good Friday a nasty prelude to Easter Sunday. (We often forget that the liturgy of Good Friday is not Jesus' funeral, but the solemn celebration of the cross's *triumph.*) In point of fact, however, Jesus' death is already the complete and unconditional surrender of a human being to the God whose goodness and love cannot be limited by a grave. Dying, Jesus forever enters the presence of that One who has never withdrawn from the world. Asleep in death on the cross, Jesus enters into a new and irreversible relationship with the God who has "disappeared" into the human world and can now be found nowhere else but there, *in* and *as* one's neighbor.

Jesus' dying and rising are thus not two separate myste- ries, but a single mystery in two "movements." That is why the New Testament very clearly insists that Jesus really died—he didn't merely faint or seem to die—and thus that the resurrection is not a resuscitation (a return to former life in the manner of Lazarus), but a radically new movement into God's endless mercy and presence. For Jesus, as for us, death brings personal history and freedom to completion, places him in the immediate presence of God and brings him into intimate, unrestricted relationship with all the world. And because for Jesus, as for us, death and resurrection are phases of a single process, each must interpret the other. Jesus' surrender to the Holy One in death ("Into your hands I commend my spirit") simultaneously signals God's complete and irrevocable acceptance (vindication) of that death. And just as Jesus' bodily humanness is part of that one world into which God's goodness and presence has forever "disappeared," so that body's glorification by the power of God (a process affirmed but never fully described in the New Testament) signals the beginning of the whole world's glorification. Gerard Manley Hopkins was uncannily accurate when he wrote,

> The world is charged with the grandeur of God.
>   It will flame out, like shining from shook foil;
>   It gathers to a greatness, like the ooze of oil
> Crushed . . .[48]

And accurate, too, was Edith Sitwell in her wonderful paraphrase of the "honey doctrine" from the *Upanishads:*

> This Earth is the honey of all Beings, and all Beings
> Are the honey of this Earth . . . O bright immortal Lover
> That is incarnate in the body's earth—
> O bright immortal Lover who is All . . .[49]

In more formal theological terms, Karl Rahner has made this same point very beautifully;

> Through Christ's death the spiritual being which was his from the beginning, and which he gave active expression to in the *life* that was completed by his death, became open to the whole world . . . became a permanent . . . modification of the world in its root and ground. . . . But this has made the world as a whole and as the scene of human activity a different place from what it would be had Christ not died: . . . possibilities now exist for the personal acts of *all* other men [and women] which would not exist but for the death of the Lord. . . . Part of the innermost being of the world is what we call Jesus Christ in his life and death, that which was poured forth upon the whole world at the moment when the vessel of his body broke in death and Christ really became, even in his humanity, what of right he always was, the heart of the world, the inmost centre of all created being.[50]

To sum it up, Jesus' death (or more precisely, his death-and-resurrection) restored death's meaning as a *human* experience with cosmic consequences. His death made it possible for us to experience and embrace our own—as gift, as surrender, as falling into the hands of eternal Mystery. While death remains something humanly suffered (and hence surrounded by pain and loss, doubt and obscurity), it can now, also, be something *done*. Once again we can turn to Karl Rahner for a deeper understanding of what this means:

> In the case of one man, the first of all, we are bold enough to believe that he was not merely made subject to death, not merely swallowed up by the absurdity of existence. Rather he himself died. *He made death his own act.* He himself assumes that which is beyond all human conception and control, and himself enacts what has to be suffered. This first one, whom we seek to follow in death, is Jesus. He died as we shall die: in that darkness into which he uttered that groan. . . . "My God, my God, why hast thou forsaken me?" In his death everything which makes death terrible took place, and that which death entails was truly suffered: the agony of the body, the brutal injustice . . . the hatred of his enemies and their mocking self-assurance, the failure of his life-work, the betrayal of his friends, and over and above all . . . that sense of futility [which happens whenever one dies in the presence of friends] who cannot help . . . the struggle for breath . . . the pain from which no one returns . . . the sense of being powerless.[51]

By restoring death to its full stature as a human deed, Jesus opened the way for all of us to embrace the cross and experience the resurrection. Here at last we can understand the connection between cross and table. For as Paul insisted in his first letter to the church at Corinth, "As often as you eat this bread and drink the cup, you proclaim the *death* of the Lord until he comes" (1 Corinthians 11:26). This passage has probably puzzled most of us at one time or another, but now we can begin to see its significance. What Jesus brought to the table is the same thing we bring: a life brought to completion in death—a death experienced as darkness, groaning, terror, agony, injustice, hatred, failure, mockery, betrayal, futility, pain and powerlessness, *and* as surrender, trust, fulfillment, gift, grace, union with the world and presence of God. Jesus destroyed death by returning it to its human roots, by letting it be what it was intended to be—the *fulfillment* of our personal freedom (which, brought fully to birth in death, can now no longer be lost); the *meeting* with a nameless Mystery whose strength surpasses both defiant despair and illusory self-sufficiency; the *beginning* of a new and limitless relationship with a world-in-process-of-glorification.

Death is what Jesus laid on the table: death for all to see and acknowledge; death ritually embodied in broken bread and poured-out wine; death as human deed, restored and redeemed by the heart of God; death as the beginning of the world's transformation, blossoming from the body of One who, dead and rising, lives wholly and immediately for God (see Romans 6:9–10). Because it celebrates the death of Jesus, *the table welcomes all human beings as equal partners in the Mystery of God.* The only requirement for admission to the table is the freedom to be human—which is, ultimately, the freedom to die.

This was the outrageous scandal of Jesus' enacted parable at table. All anyone had to bring to it was the power to die. This meant that all the rules are broken, all the boundaries transgressed. This meant that the power of religious potentates to decide who is worthy to eat and drink in the kingdom of God is defeated. This meant that God's mercy stretches as wide as the miserable and marginalized, the outcast and stigmatized. This meant equal partnership for all at table—and an end to privileged places, persons and perks. This meant that God can no longer be imagined as a Patriarch who underwrites the proprietary claims of men over women. This meant that God's ways are not our ways, that God's name and nature is being redefined, that religious faith is being totally renegotiated and set upon a new footing.

For many of Jesus' associates, such views were not only unimaginably brash, they constituted a prostitution of devout believers' deepest hopes. To welcome outcasts to table-companionship *in the name of God's reign*—in the name of a people's supreme religious hopes—not only called traditional faith into question, it also "shattered the closed ranks of the community against their enemy."[52] (Recall what was said above about the table's role in establishing group identity, prestige and membership boundaries.) To eat with sinners and tax collectors (who represented religious and political oppression) was to become one of them, to connive with the enemy. To welcome them back to the community table (indiscriminately, in the name of the community's highest hope!) was to violate every canon of accepted belief and decent behavior.

Yet this is exactly what Jesus did. The table became the place where anyone "bound for death" could experience forgiveness—could step over the line from *living the past* (the reign of sin and Satan, the reign of all that is impervious to God's grace and presence) to *living the present-future* (the arrival of God in this very moment of history). Norman Perrin summarized the point this way:

> The central feature of the message of Jesus is . . . the challenge of the forgiveness of sins and the offer of the possibility of a new kind of relationship with God and with one's fellow [humans]. This was symbolized by a table-fellowship which celebrated the present joy and anticipated the future consummation; a table-fellowship of such joy and gladness that it survived the crucifixion and provided the focal point for the community life of the earliest Christians, and was the most direct link between that community life and the pre-Easter fellowship of Jesus and his disciples. . . . We are justified in seeing this table-fellowship as the central feature of the ministry of Jesus; an anticipatory sitting at table in the Kingdom of God and a very real celebration of present joy and challenge.[53]

The rood of dreams became a table of dreams. For both cross and meal had the same purpose: healing, reconciliation, bonding among all those whose elbows rest on the same wood, whose hands break the same bread, whose lips draw comfort from the same cup. As Doris Donnelly has so aptly put it,

> Reconciliation is God's dream for the world. It involves restoring broken relationships, healing our deepest wounds, and transforming hearts in the peace of Christ.
>
> Reconciliation cannot happen unless we come to terms with the alienation we experience with our divided selves, with each other, and even with God. The duty of the ambassador is not to run from the horror of alienation but rather to match its potential for destruction and despair with the life and hope of reconciliation.[54]

A table of dreams. Human history is, more than anything else, a history of food—of what happens (or fails to happen) around a table. (Even the Bible begins with forbidden food in a garden and ends with festal food at the Lamb's banquet in a New City.) Indeed, a strong case can be made that to learn the ritual repertoire of a people (as embodied, especially, in its table etiquette) is to learn the arts of becoming human. For as Herbert Fingarette once argued, human community *is* holy rite.[55] Our deepest human relationships do not just happen; they are cultivated, cherished, cared for and cared about. Our relations are ceremonialized, from the almost imperceptible micro-greetings exchanged by passersby on a sidewalk to the solemn cortege that bears a body to its burial place. In her wonderful book *The Rituals of Dinner,* Margaret Visser highlights these points:

> Rituals are there to make difficult passages easier. They include the gestures—waving, nodding, smiling, speaking set phrases—which daily smooth our meetings with other people; the attitudes and postures we adopt when standing or sitting in the presence of others, especially when we are talking to them; the muttering of "excuse me" when interrupting others or squeezing past them. *Full-dress celebrations of coming together, of marking transitions and recollections, almost always require food,* with all the ritual politeness implied in dining—the proof that we all know how eating should be managed. We eat whenever life becomes dramatic: at weddings, birthdays, funerals, at parting and at

welcoming home, or at any moment which a group decides is worthy of remark. . . .

Food is still our ritual relaxation (a "break" in the working day), our chance to choose our companions and talk to them, the excuse to re-create our humanity as well as our strength, and to renew our relationships.[56]

Food is "our chance to choose our companions." Once again, the shocking thing about Jesus' table manners was not simply that he chose to eat with the wrong kind of people, but that he embraced the chance to eat with anybody in the name of God's reign. Jesus chose *everyone* as a privileged table companion, welcomed all comers—not just some of them. He recognized that God's dream of reconciliation touches high and low, saint and sinner, the devout and the dissipated, all that is human and all that is beyond the human. One is reminded of the famous homily by John Chrysostom which is read in the Byzantine liturgy on Easter Sunday morning:

Let all the pious, let all lovers of God
    rejoice in the splendor of this feast! . . .
Come, all of you, and enter into the joy of your Lord.
You the first and you the last: Receive alike your reward!
You the rich and you the poor: Dance together!
You sober and you weaklings: Celebrate the day!
You who kept the fast and you who didn't: Rejoice today!
The table is richly loaded: Enjoy its royal banquet!
The calf is a fatted one: *Let no one go away hungry!*
All of you enjoy the banquet of faith;
All of you receive the riches of God's goodness.[57]

The only thing we need bring to God's table is the ability to die (as Jesus did, surrounded by doubts and questions, by suffering and sorrow—and finally, by surrender and self-forgetting). Dying, we arrive at the table of dreams, where all humanity is gathered and the world's transfiguration is begun. In his famous meditation "The Mass on the World," the great Jesuit paleontologist Pierre Teilhard de Chardin gives us a vision of what this table-sharing by a transfigured humanity in a transfigured cosmos might resemble:

It is done.
Once again the Fire has penetrated the earth . . .
Without earthquake, or thunderclap,
the flame has lit up the whole world from within.
All things individually and collectively are penetrated
and flooded by it,
from the inmost core of the tiniest atom
to the mighty sweep of the most universal laws of being . . .
In the new humanity which is begotten today
the Word prolongs the unending act of birth;
and by virtue of the Word's immersion
into the world's womb,
the great waters of the kingdom of matter have,
without even a ripple, been endued with life. . . .
Through your own incarnation, my God,
all matter is henceforth incarnate. . . .

Glorious Lord Christ—
the Divine Influence,
secretly diffused and active in the depths of matter;
Dazzling Center,
where all the innumerable fibres of the manifold meet;
Power,
as implacable as the world and as warm as life—
You whose forehead is of the whiteness of snow,
whose eyes are of fire
and whose feet are brighter than molten gold;
You whose hands imprison the stars;
You who are the first and the last,
the living and the dead and the risen again;
You who gather into your exuberant unity every beauty,
every affinity, every energy, every mode of existence;
it is you to whom my being cried out,
with a desire as vast as the universe,
"In truth, You are my Lord and my God!"[58]

In the next chapter we shall look more closely at this table of dreams to which death—our *human* death, our *baptismal* death—has brought us. For after all the soul-searching of conversion, after all the patient probing of precatechumenate, after all the rites of enrollment, election and scrutiny, after all the water and washing and anointing, *table* is the place that the process takes us. Jesus' call to conversion is a call to come to the table, and table is the place where the Lord's death—and our own—is proclaimed. Table is the place where the Great Dance begins and ends; where the Tree planted in *that* world ripens in *this;* where the fountain that sprang with mingled blood and life in the Dark World flows here with life only.

Chapter 2

Re-creating the World

■

In *The Shape of Baptism,* his classic study of Christian initiation (its historical roots, its reform by the Second Vatican Council), Aidan Kavanagh has written:

> [Baptism] is inadequately perceptible apart from the eucharist; . . . the eucharist is not wholly knowable without reference to conversion in faith; . . . conversion is abortive if it does not issue in sacramental illumination by incorporation into the church; . . . the church is only an inept corporation without steady access to Sunday, Lent, the Easter Vigil; . . . evangelization is mere noise and catechesis only a syllabus apart from conversion and initiation into a robust ecclesial environment of faith shared. *In baptism the eucharist begins, and in the eucharist baptism is sustained. From this premier sacramental union flows all the church's life.*[1]

In a word, eucharist is the concluding act in that ensemble of rites we call "Christian initiation" precisely because it is the abiding, embodied ritual symbol of all that it means to live and die as a Christian. Kavanagh notes,

47

> The eucharist is . . . most profoundly the constantly reiterated "seal" of baptism, as baptism is its unique and unrepeatable introit. The eucharist, being the way baptism always comes to rest with Catholic Christians throughout their lives, is unavoidably the sacrament of Christian maturity. For this reason it is the eucharist that ends the sequence of sacramental initiation, not confirmation. Confirmation "seals" baptism in such a manner that thereafter the eucharist is not only a rite but a Spirit-filled way of corporate life in the Body of Christ which is the church.[2]

Because it is not just a rite but a way of life, because it celebrates not the past but the present coming-to-be of this assembly as church, because it announces not so much who we are as who we are to become in the full and final presence of God's reign, the eucharist is the climax of all those acts and processes by which human persons are called "out of darkness into God's wonderful light" (1 Peter 2:9). That this is the case is clear if one reflects for a moment on the structure and shape of the Easter Vigil. The vigil is not simply one rite among many, but the condition of possibility for all the rest. On that "most blessed of all nights" we gather not nostalgically, to remember our roots, but *ritually,* to re-create the world. As Gail Ramshaw has reminded us, what the Easter Vigil proposes "is not memory, but metaphor; not pilgrimage, but liturgy."[3] The vigil is thus a night of hard work wherein we undertake the construction of a new world and a new humanity.

First, the Conflagration

The vigil begins, as it were, with an act of ritual arson. We light this fire not because spring nights are chilly, not because our pagan ancestors greeted the equinox with bonfires on hillsides, not even because our forbears in faith were led by "a pillar of cloud by day, a pillar of fire by night" — but because *kindling a fire is a daring, dangerous and destructive thing to do.* The world as we know it has to be torched. (Local fire marshals, take note! We're doing this on purpose! Arrest us if you dare!) The fire is to the vigil what the Big Bang was to the universe: an explosion so uncontrollably vast in its magnitude, so awesome in its energy, so fierce in its power to destroy and create, that light and radiation from it are still not spent these billions of years later. A fire (a roaring, raging fire, not a timid tea candle) is lit at the beginning of the Easter night because unless everything we know is destroyed, nothing will ever really change. On this night we say to the world as we know it:

> Are you willing to be sponged out, erased, canceled,
>   made nothing?
> Are you willing to be made nothing?
> dipped into oblivion?
>
> If not, you will never really change.
>
> The phoenix renews her youth
> only when she is burnt, burnt alive, burnt down
> to hot and flocculent ash.[4]

Destroying all that we've ever known, fire also *creates* something new and potentially as hazardous. As long as the "world as we know it" endured, "business as usual" could survive, and we could continue our careers as unrepentant predators—welcoming the night's isolation, feeding our bodies (and our egos) on the day's kill, licking our wounds and plotting revenge. But as soon as we humans learned how to make fire, we destroyed the familiar world of predatory competition and created a world of social cooperation. Fire did more than warm, enlighten or protect: It made it possible for human *individuals* to become human *communities*. As anthropologist Richard Leakey has remarked,

> Not only did [fire] provide warmth . . . *it also stretched social intercourse into the hours of darkness,* a time when the hearth would be the focus of the social group. So, as the flames were keeping potential predators at bay, they were also drawing people together, giving an opportunity for telling stories and creating myths and rituals.[5]

In short, fire forced us to deal with each other, forced us to surrender egocentric isolation, forced us to let our lives and

49

fortunes be changed—changed utterly—by the presence and experience of others. With the advent of fire as a human technology (and not merely as a capricious accident of nature), we could no longer slink off into our caves alone, could no longer avoid social bonds and contracts. Not only were we forced to surrender nocturnal silence in favor of stories shared around a flickering fire, we were also forced to add a crucial element to our primitive nutritional repertoire. From now on, food no longer had to be raw or rotting (transformations wrought by nature)—it could be cooked (a transformation wrought by culinary culture).

So fire also forced us to deal with food in new ways. Notice that the Easter Vigil begins with the ritual rediscovery of precisely that technology which makes the final act of the night possible: the sharing of a meal. What lies on the table is not wheat and grapes but bread and wine, items created by fermentation and fire, by processes of creative destruction instigated by human agents for human purposes. What lies on the table is culture, not nature. What lies there is fragrant with the musky pungency of human intervention.

This bread that on the table lies, moreover, is acknowledged as meat, as flesh. For though it may grieve the vegetarians among us, the fact that we humans became carnivores, meat-eaters, was crucial to the development of dining and table-companionship. Fruits, nuts and vegetables are packaged so neatly by nature that they don't need or promote communal acts of gathering and eating. But meat did—and still does. Its hunting, killing, dressing and consumption require repeated acts of cooperation and social bonding. The eating of meat may also have provoked a primal crisis of conscience, a moral dilemma, for our species. We found, to our horror, that we could live only by killing other living things. As Diane Ackerman writes in her wonderful book *A Natural History of the Senses,*

> [We] must kill other forms of life in order to live. We must steal their lives, sometimes causing them great pain. Every one of us

performs or tacitly approves of small transactions with torture, death and butchery each day. . . . In our hearts, we know that life loves life. Yet we feast on some of the other life-forms with which we share our planet; we kill to live.[6]

Or, as Aidan Kavanagh has put it,

> However elegant the knowledge of the dining room may be, it begins in the soil, in the barnyard, in the slaughterhouse; amid the quiet violence of the garden, strangled cries, and fat spitting in the pan. Table manners depend on something's having been grabbed by the throat.[7]

Second, the Words Around the Fire

Not only did we humans make fire to make food; we made it to be encircled by our bodies and our words. Circling fire gave us both shared space and shared stories. This burning ring created the possibility not only of a culinary culture, but of an oral and auditory one as well. No longer was human experience closeted and incommunicable. Rather, it could be remembered and retold, edited and embellished, or hidden and withheld.

So fire forced us to become storytellers, mythographers who could map the world's meanings—and transmit them to others with tongue and breath, brush and hand. For the stories we tell are not only spoken and heard, they are drawn. The first human stories of record were those painted more than 17,000 years ago on the walls of caves in places like Lascaux, where our archaic ancestors—wishing to tell us what was most human about themselves—chose to paint not portraits of faces but portraits of hands. Hands were the first storytellers; they learned to draw the very sounds that made the stories. Alphabets display us humans as creatures who still think with our skins and remember with our bodies, as wizards who make words not only audible but visible.

As audible sounds and visible signs, stories shared around the fire gave us the ability to re-create the world at will— **51** enlarging and exaggerating *this* detail; silencing *that* memory; turning time on its head by taking events out of sequence; editing images so as to blur the divisions between desire and dream, deceit and truth, the real and the imagined. If fire forced us to deal in new ways with people and food, stories liberated us from the cruel tyranny of "plain facts." At the Easter Vigil, Christians re-create the world mythographically, repeating ancient stories in ever-new contexts, and thereby "redeeming the time" by remaking it.

Third, the Water

In its first two movements, the Easter Vigil re-creates the world through fire and word. In its third, it re-creates the world through water. Again, the reasons for this have everything to do with our origins and evolution as a species. For human beings, water means mobility. If it's in short supply, we move to find it, to be near it; if it's superabundant, we move to get away from its flooding force. The history of human change and movement is the history of its relation to water. Tribal migrations, choices of sites for fields and flocks, cities and villages—all are determined by water's absence or presence. Even temple and cult depended upon an adequate water supply, as Joachim Jeremias has shown in his study of Jerusalem at the time of Jesus.[8]

Like fire and word, water plays on the ambiguous relation between nature and culture. Water's *nature* cannot be controlled or contained by human choice. Rain falls where and when it wills; rivers flood according to their own schedules, without regard for the convenience of those who dwell along their banks. In human hands, however, water becomes a technological tool, a creature of *culture*. By nature it can't be carried; but we make it a companion for our travels, a portable commodity. When it doesn't flow in the direction we want, we build a dam and change its course. When it doesn't reach our fifth-floor flat or our fiftieth-floor office, we defy gravity's pull and pump it upward till it gushes in force from faucets and taps. And by so doing we stretch the limits of our world, exponentially expanding our choices for movement and change.

As nature, then, water may kill or give life—as rain it can save a city; as a *tsunami* it can destroy a population. But as culture, water is wedded to human purpose. Like the circle of fire and the repeated cycle of stories, it forces us to renegotiate all our relationships—with the earth, hence with one another, hence with God. Water becomes the coinage of human commerce, a medium for our most critical transactions, both intimate and public. From having sex to having babies; from personal hygiene to public hydrants; from baptizing to blessing; from washing cars to washing feet; water signals both the *presence* of humans and their *power* to change relationships. (For, as I suggested earlier, water means mobility—not just physical and spatial mobility, but inward, interpersonal, spiritual and psychological movement as well. How often, indeed, water floods not only our basements but our dreams!)

In the baptismal waters of the Easter Vigil, then, the world is renamed and re-created—not only for the neophyte but for the whole assembly of believers. Just as human hands reshape words as art in alphabets (so that stories are not merely told but painted), so hands reconfigure water (creating human habitats out of inhuman waste). In the waters of the vigil a new map of the world is drawn. (The old rubrics graphically portrayed this, for the presider was instructed to ruffle the water's stillness, breathing upon it as it was blessed—dividing and parting it with his hand, and striking it with the candle—a mythological "magic wand" if ever there was one!) Old barriers are broken; new boundaries appear. The landscape of the celebrating assembly is changed forever as a new and terrible beauty is born. As the early Christian bishop Zeno of Verona (died circa 371 CE) said to those about to be baptized into the death and rising of Jesus:

Oh yes, brothers and sisters, you are on fire with a thirst that can never be quenched! The sweet murmur of flowing nectar beckons you. Rush! Suck the milk from this genital font! Drink deeply, while there is still time! Let the water's waves wash over you. With all your energy and devotion, fill your vessels now — so that you will always have enough water. For remember this, above all: If ever you spill a drop, you can't return to fetch it again![9]

And Finally, the Food

As flood follows fire, so food follows flood in the unfolding of the Easter Vigil. Because the world as we know it has been torched; because its map has been redrawn by word and water; because all our relationships have been reconfigured by flood and font, we survivors must learn new ways to feed ourselves. We do this by engaging in an utterly new form of dining that has come to be known, in our tradition, as "eucharist."

Overfamiliarity, of course, has blunted our perception of what a radical departure this eucharistic feasting is from other forms of feeding. (Indeed, it will be this chapter's chief purpose to reacquaint readers with the awesome and revolutionary *newness* of Jesus' approach to table-partnership.) For the moment, however, I simply want to call attention to the fact that eucharist is the final act in the Easter Vigil's recreation of the world.

Earlier I noted that what lies on the Lord's table are not merely nature's gifts — but *nature's gifts as transformed by human hands.* As a human commodity, food is never simply "natural" (all the contemporary interest in organic gardening, macrobiotic diets and nutritional purity notwithstanding). It is always tangled in a web of work and worry, affections and emotions. Even the very first food we taste — the colostrum from our mother's breast that bears her whole immunological history — is, as Diane Ackerman has written, accompanied by love and affection, stroking, a sense of security, warmth and well-being, our first intense feelings of pleasure. Later on she will feed us solid food from her hands, or even chew food first and press it into our mouths, partially digested. Such powerful associations do not fade easily, if at all. We say "food" as if it were a simple thing, an absolute like rock or rain. . . . But it is a big source of pleasure in most lives, a complex realm of satisfaction both physiological and emotional, much of which involves memories of childhood. Food must taste good, must reward us, or we would not stoke the furnace in each of our cells. We must eat to live; it takes energy and planning, so it must tantalize us out of our natural torpor.[10]

What lies on the table—*any* table—is never just food. What lies there is always a complex history of hunting and hording, testing and tasting, seduction, skill and sex, "a jungle of sweet temptations." Recall Sophia Loren's famous quip, "All you see here I owe to spaghetti." Or recall the sumptuous scene in the film *Babette's Feast:* Though the guests have conspired to dislike the food Babette prepares, they find themselves overpowered by the provocative pleasures of taste. With each bite their expectations rise, until they are utterly seduced into new ways of experiencing food—and hence, of relating to each other. For taste, as Diane Ackerman reminds us, is "an intimate sense; we can't taste things at a distance":

Should an alien civilization ever contact us, the greatest gift they could give us would be a set of home movies: films of our species at each stage in our evolution. Consciousness, the great poem of matter, seems so unlikely, so impossible, and yet here we are with our loneliness and our giant dreams. Speaking into the perforations of a telephone receiver as if through the screen of a confessional, we do sometimes share our emotions with a friend, but usually this is too disembodied, too much like yelling into the wind. We prefer to talk *in person,* as if we could temporarily slide into their feelings. Our friend first offers us food, drink. It is a symbolic act, a gesture that says: *This food will nourish your body as I will nourish your soul.* In hard times, or in the wild, it also says *I will endanger my own life by parting with some of what I must consume to survive.* Those desperate times may be ancient history, but the part of us forged in such trials accepts the token drink and piece of cheese and is grateful.[11]

On the table, then—*any* table—there is never just food. There is, rather, the whole history of creation struggling toward consciousness, of peripheries pushing toward a center, of stone seeking speech, of wood waiting for something or someone to carry. On the table—*any* table—lies a staggering history of needs felt, met or denied; of stammered confessions; of hands groping for the last crust of bread; of goblets glowing, lifted and struck; of accusations and reprieves; of lost children and drowned lovers. There are luscious pears that first ripened seven centuries ago in Anjou—whose branch and blossom, perhaps, touched the cheek of Eleanor of Aquitaine. There are sugar-snap peas whose rightful place in the sun and soil was guaranteed by the patient hands of anonymous Guatemalan women. There are cardamom, ginseng and peppercorns—spices for which, centuries ago, colorful caravans of Italian merchants made pilgrimage to India and Cathay. There are the resting arms of homeless elders about to celebrate their last suppers. There are the tightly twined fingers of the anxious or the agonized. The surface of every table holds a rich patina of sighs, tears, betrayals, deaths, debts and promises—of which, indeed, food is the abiding symbol.

How right, then, was poet Pablo Neruda to note that the simplest of the foods we share enfolds the whole history of our species. Speaking of "the apogee of celery," Neruda wrote:

> Fibers of darkness and weeping light,
> blind embellishments, curly energies,
> river of life and essential fibers,
> green branches of cherished sun,
> here I am, in the night, listening to secrets,
> wakefulness, solitudes,
> and you enter, amid the sunken fog,
> until you grow in me, until you reveal to me
> the dark light and the rose of the earth.[12]

Laid on the table, a simple rib of celery, broken from the stalk, becomes a scented chest of secrets, memories, energies and risks.

To come to the table, then, is to come bearing in one's body an awesome history of remembered taste, pleasure, husbandry, violence, cruelty and sacrifice. At table, there are no innocents: Blood and dirt cover every hand and all have need of mercy. Arrived at this point, we must do what fire did in the Vigil's first movement. We must torch and abandon "the world as we know it," and find in food another world, newborn and salted—a world in which, because all have need of mercy, each of us says to the other: *"I will endanger my own life by parting with some of what I must consume to survive. I will be breath of your breath and bone of your bone. I will be the blood that flows to meet your desire, the body that rises to meet your hunger."*

Fire, story, water and food: These are the elements that made us *us.* Our ability to transport them made it possible for us to become the conscious, cooperative, culture-making creatures that we are. We carry the same four commodities into the Easter Vigil, where we ritually review, renegotiate, renew and reenact all the passages that make us human: the perilous passage from *beast* (aware only of God) to *beauty* (aware of God and itself); the painful passage from *immolated* to *immolator;* the ponderous passage from creation's *consciousness* to creation's *conscience.* In making those passages, we re-create the world. No one leaves the Easter Vigil the same. If you do, you haven't been there.

The Social World of Jesus

I began this chapter with a meditation on the way the Easter Vigil re-creates the world because if we are to grasp Jesus' eucharistic teaching—and its radical significance as the act that completes Christian initiation—we must come to grips with the world in which he lived and the ways he subverted that world through the fellowship of the table. **57**

In the past few years biblical scholarship has benefited enormously from insights developed by the social sciences, especially cultural anthropology and cross-cultural studies. Especially valuable have been the perspectives gained from the study of Mediterranean culture during the time of Jesus. All generalizations, of course, are somewhat misleading, for while the ancient Mediterranean world was climatically and ecologically homogeneous (characterized by extended summer droughts and mild rainy winters favorable to the growth of such crops as wheat, olives and vines, and by sharp contrasts between mountainous topography and fertile agricultural valleys), this obviously does not mean that all its peoples thought, lived and behaved in identical ways. Still, it is increasingly clear to scholars that the social world of that place and period differed in decisive ways from our own. Here, it will be useful to summarize some of the characteristics of ancient Mediterranean culture, especially as it colored views of self and society, power and prestige.

An Agrarian Society Virtually all Mediterranean societies, as anthropologist David Gilmore has noted, were "undercapitalized agrarian civilizations":

> They are characterized by sharp social stratification and by both a relative and absolute scarcity of natural resources. . . . There is little social mobility. Power is highly concentrated in a few hands, and the bureaucratic functions of the state are poorly developed. . . . These conditions are of course ideal for the development of patron-client ties and a dependency ideology.[13]

In a word, Mediterranean society was characterized by sharp social contrasts. Gilmore speaks of "a polarized agrarian dualism of scale," that is, great estates (representing commercial farming on a large and prosperous scale) alternated with tiny subsistence plots (worked by peasants). It was also characterized—as we shall see below—by intense competition between agriculture (crop farming) and pastoralism (livestock breeding and raising).

Urban Orientation   While agriculture was the principal economic backbone of Mediterranean life, the significance of urban centers should not be underestimated. In point of fact, the strong urban orientation of that world resulted, as Gilmore notes, in

> a corresponding disdain for the peasant way of life and for manual labor; sharp social, geographic, and economic stratification; political instability; . . . "atomistic" community life; rigid sexual segregation, a tendency toward reliance on the smallest possible kinship units (nuclear families and shallow lineages); strong emphasis on shifting, ego-centered, noncorporate coalitions; an honor-and-shame syndrome which defines both sexuality and personal reputation.[14]

One should note here that although Jesus himself has often been imagined as a kind of simple, small-town peasant — a "good country boy" — such an image is largely without foundation in fact. The Galilee of Jesus' day cannot be viewed as simply an unimportant and isolated backwater. Indeed, during the first century CE, southern (or "lower") Galilee — where Jesus' hometown of Nazareth was located — was one of the most densely populated regions of the Roman Empire. Its numerous villages, towns and cities were packed together in an area roughly 15 by 25 miles. Andrew Overman writes,

> One is never more than a day's walk from anywhere in lower Galilee. One could not live in any village in lower Galilee and escape the effects and ramifications of urbanization. . . . Life in lower Galilee in the first century was as urbanized and urbane as anywhere else in the empire.[15]

Nazareth, in fact, was a mere three or four miles from Sepphoris, an aristocratic Jewish city that became, during the reign of Herod Antipas (ca. 4 BCE – 39 CE), the administrative center of the Roman provincial government. In short, Jesus grew up within a densely populated urban area where even smaller villages (like Nazareth) — though they might be conservative and Aramaic-speaking — shared common cultural ground with larger, hellenized (and often

Greek-speaking) cities. Neither Jesus nor his earliest followers were innocent country yokels who lacked all acquaintance with urban manners and mores. On the contrary, they were people who grew up in the very shadow of Sepphoris—a city that the Jewish historian Josephus called "the ornament of all Galilee," and which served through most of Jesus' lifetime as a bustling provincial capital. With its location along a busy trade route, its large public buildings (including a theater), its sophisticated Jewish community and its sizable contingent of imperial officers and bureaucrats, Sepphoris was clearly a city to be reckoned with, an important regional center of commerce, government, religious and cultural life. And Jesus apparently lived no more than an easy morning's walk away from it.

Social Structure   The primary forms of social stratification in ancient Mediterranean culture arose chiefly from three sources: *class,* determined by riches and property or the lack thereof; *bureaucracy,* a brokered system of clients and patrons; and the *ideological hierarchy of honor and shame.* Each of these was related more or less directly to *wealth*—its unequal distribution; its control by the few; its guaranteed access to power, privilege and prestige (hence the hierarchies established by patronage and brokerage, honor and shame). And wealth, in its turn, was determined largely by what Jane Schneider has called "a highly competitive relationship between *agricultural* and *pastoral* economies, under pressure from urban centers and in the absence of effective state institutions."[16]

Because of its ecological circumstances, therefore, the Mediterranean world was an extremely paradoxical one, "a friendly sea surrounded by a hostile landscape." In some areas, extreme aridity (the Arabian and Saharan deserts) or hilly and mountainous terrain (lower Galilee) favored pastoralism. But there were also vast stretches of the

Mediterranean basin that (as noted above) favored agriculture. As a result, there was constant bickering and tension between the interests of flocks and fields, between breeders of livestock and producers of wheat, grapes and olives. As Jane Schneider notes,

> [P]astoralism in the Mediterranean was challenged by the continuous expansion of agriculture. . . . Because transport by sea was easy, Iron Age technologies for the production of agricultural surpluses diffused into dry and mountainous zones which might otherwise have remained pastoral, broken only by scattered communities of marginal, autochthonous cultivators. Particularly on the less arid European side, landlords devoted vast regions to the production of wheat for export, simply because of the facility with which it could be transported by sea.[17]

Two fundamental factors, then, supported the social strata of the ancient Mediterranean world: *competition* and *inequality*. Competition within local communities (and not simply between social or economic classes) was a tremendously important feature—especially of rural life. Ordinarily this competition focused on strategic—but scarce—resources such as water, tillable land, pastures for grazing livestock and access routes to land. From time immemorial, observes Jane Schneider,

> Mediterranean peoples have quarreled over encroachments on boundaries, usurpations of water rights, abusive pasturing, animal theft, the destruction of crops, adultery, and murder. They consider such violations as challenges to the honor of the property holding group. Thus *honor can be thought of as the ideology of a property holding group which struggles to define, enlarge and protect its patrimony in a competitive arena.*[18]

More will be said later about this ideology of honor and shame, especially as it affects interpersonal relationships. For the moment, it is important simply to note that crucial aspects of social structure in the ancient Mediterranean world resulted from conflict between agricultural and pastoral interests, and from competition within communities over access to vital resources. Further, there were no strongly developed state agencies to resolve such local, intracommunitarian conflicts. Most of the Mediterranean region, indeed, was hostile to any and all attempts at administrative supervision. Such conditions encouraged local groups to invent their own techniques of social control through codes of honor and shame, as well as through informal but potent systems of patronage:

> In much of the Mediterranean, pastoralism and agriculture coexisted, competing for the same resources in a way which fragmented the social organization of each type of community and blurred the boundary between them. In the absence of the state, pastoral communities, and agricultural communities in their midst, developed their own means of social control—the codes of honor and shame—which were adapted to the intense conflict that external pressures had created within them, and between them.[19]

Inequality—institutionalized inequality—was the second great principle of Mediterranean political life and social organization. Indeed, the very survival of both the honor-and-shame ideology and the patron-and-client hierarchy depended (as we shall see) on maintaining conditions of economic, social and political inequality—just as they depended on maintaining weak administrative control at the state level and the continuation of competitive, atomized social relations at the local level. If honor is "the ideology of a property holding group," then its survival obviously depends on keeping in place the sharp distinction between prosperous property owners and impoverished peasants. If patronage exists to broker relations between "haves" and "have-nots," then its persistence depends on keeping inequalities intact.

In a word, the survival of ancient Mediterranean culture depended on ongoing competition between sheep-herders and farmers, on keeping the landless poor in their place, on maintaining the system of clients' dependence on powerful patrons and on exerting social control through codes of honor and shame.

Social Control: Honor and Shame   As suggested in the preceding point, the modern notion of a strong national state, fully empowered to enact laws, arbitrate disputes and resolve conflicts among citizens, did not exist in the ancient Mediterranean world. Social control was exerted not by bureaucratic decisions or procedures at the national level, but by ad hoc codes and hierarchies developed within small, local, particularistic groups. In such small-scale social contexts, personal face-to-face relations are of far greater importance than anonymous, impersonal or bureaucratic ones. And where such face-to-face encounters are paramount, honor and shame become an individual's constant preoccupation. As Jane Schneider has written,

> The problem of honor becomes salient when the group is threatened with competition from equivalent groups . . . especially . . . when small . . . groups, such as families, clans or gangs, are the principal units of power, sovereign or nearly so over the territories they control. Concern for honor also grows when contested resources are subject to redivision along changing lines, when there is no stable relationship between units of power and precisely delimited patrimonies, i.e., when the determination of boundary lines is subject to continual human intervention. Finally, concern with honor arises when the definition of the group is problematic; when social boundaries are difficult to maintain and internal loyalties are questionable.
> *Shame, the reciprocal of honor, is especially important when one of the contested resources is women, and women's comportment defines the honor of social groups.* Like all ideologies, honor and shame complement institutional arrangements for the distribution of power and the creation of order in society.[20]

It is important here to observe that codes of honor and shame are characteristic of individuals whose self-perceptions are derived primarily from what others think of them, whose self-image mirrors what others see. Such individuals always look at themselves through others' eyes; they need others in order to exist, in order to grasp their own identity. Their conscience interiorizes what others think, believe and value; their self-worth depends upon the recognition, by

others, of excellence, integrity and pride. To lose honor—
to be shamed—is to lose the respect of others.

In such a system, those who lose others' respect cease to
exist socially. The shamed count for nothing, have no status,
no power, no identity. It is incumbent upon those who
hope to survive in such an honor-and-shame system constantly to assert themselves, to prove themselves worthy of
respect. This is particularly true when competition arises
within a group over three basic issues: wealth, status and
sexuality, which in these androcentric cultures means "mas-
culinity narrowly defined as virility."[21] Depending upon
which of these three issues is paramount, the meaning of
honor may vary. As a category of *status,* honor may simply
flow from the recognition, within a group of peers, that
someone possesses seniority in age and/or wisdom. As a
moral category, honor attaches to those who possess personal righteousness and probity, and who hence enjoy the
respect and esteem of others. As an *economic* category, honor
belongs to those whose wealth frees them from manual
labor (in this context, work and honor are antithetical;
leisure and honor are inseparable). As a *sexual* category,
honor connotes masculine display and predatory prowess—
in competition for power over women, one man's success is
another's failure.

It is the sexual significance of shame and honor that has
special relevance here. As John Dominic Crossan has noted,
the ideology of honor and shame in first-century Mediterranean societies was usually libidinized or eroticized, that is,
it was indissolubly linked to strategies of masculine power
over women and to androcentric control of gender relations.[22] In this libidinized social system of shame and honor,
competition for the scarcest of all "resources"—marriageable
women—took on both cultural and sexual significance.
Culturally, the competition for women created a symbolic
arena or outlet for male aggressions, serving as a displace-
ment for energies that might otherwise explode in open
hostility between villages, clans or families. Sexually, it

became an occasion for erotic boasting, display and conquest, for saving face or losing it vis-à-vis other males (on the principle that "being a man" involves cuckolding others).

Such attitudes simultaneously elevated and devalued women. On the one hand, in fragmented societies such as the ancient Mediterranean—where family lineage may be very unstable and its long-term economic interests, therefore, quite vulnerable—women are "insurance." As Jane Schneider remarks,

> The repository of family and lineage honor, the focus of common interest among the men of the family or lineage, is its women. A woman's status defines the status of all the men who are related to her in determinate ways. These men share the consequences of what happens to her, and share therefore the commitment to protect her virtue. She is part of their patrimony.[23]

This may explain why, in the social world of Jesus' time, the virginal purity of a potential wife and mother played such a pivotal role in negotiations for a marriage. In a real and radical sense, a family's honor and its future depended upon the purity, loyalty and fertility of *this* woman. At the same time, such concerns about women reveal why infighting among in-laws was so legendary. For, after all, daughters were given in marriage precisely to those competing groups with whom the father of the bride had conflicts. A marriage thus represented intensely ambivalent relations between families: affinity and hostility. But the obvious intention of intermarriage (and hence the concern for the quality and integrity of women) was to control and limit the hostility through the economic and social expediency of joined bloodlines.

Despite their importance for a family's future, however, women could be—and routinely were—devalued in traditional Mediterranean societies. For although women's comportment defined and guaranteed family honor, women themselves were often denounced and demonized as treacherously unstable, inferior beings. Indeed, as Jane Schneider notes, it was widely assumed that women are victims of

65

their own sexual powers, that they are lascivious temptresses and thus potential traitors to the family household—"devil's nets," as the Arabs put it.[24] Thus, in some Mediterranean societies, the men identify themselves as *sheep* (descended from God), while the women are identified as *goats* (descended from the devil). Repeatedly, women's "ungovernable sexuality" (evident especially in their uncontrollable monthly flow of menstrual blood) is viewed by males with anxiety and fear. Women are thus perceived as symbols of chaos and disorder—outsiders, strangers, a "foreign sex."[25]

To sum it up, the ideology of honor and shame supported a system of gender-based, male-dominated social relations that both idolized women (as defenders of family honor, as emblems of virginal purity) and kept them subservient and silent (through relative seclusion, severely restricted access to public life, lowered eyes, conservative clothing, etc.). It was, as Crossan has observed, an ideology

> of small . . . unstable groups competing permanently for basic resources that are attained insecurely and maintained precariously but where conflict must be reluctantly transposed into cooperation for the most precious resource of all, marriageable women.[26]

As a loosely constructed, family-based system of morals and values, the honor-and-shame ideology was always threatened by social instability—especially by competition from other families of shepherds or farmers; by competition for scarce or contested resources; and by assaults on the family's boundaries (from internal or external sources). Given such assumptions, one can understand how radical—and how liberating—the early Christian affirmation of egalitarianism sounded: "There is neither Jew nor Greek, there is neither slave nor free person, there is neither male nor female; for you are all one in Christ Jesus" (Galatians 3:28, a formula that may have had its origins in primitive baptismal catechesis and liturgy).

Social Control: Patrons and Clients   A second form of social control found in ancient Mediterranean cultures was the system of patronage, a kind of good-old-boy network of favors and rewards rooted in the ideology of shame and honor. David Gilmore has pointed out that, in the various Mediterranean models of patronage, three ingredients consistently appear:

1) Relations between patron and client are always *asymmetrical* in terms of wealth and power. "The patron always has access to resources legally denied the client."[27]

2) *Reciprocity* and *interdependence* always characterize the exchange between patron and client: The client needs a favor, but the patron also needs something of value (votes, perhaps, or information).

3) *Informality* marks the patron-client relationship. Because there is great reluctance to leave a "paper trail," arrangements are rarely committed to writing. It should be noted, too, that negotiations between patrons and clients were usually brokered, and hence *indirect*. Brokers (the "middlemen" in the patronage system) thus served as clients to powerful patrons and as patrons to less powerful and subordinate clients. It was, in short, a system that provided "consistent ideological support for social inequality and dependency throughout the Mediterranean area."[28]

What conditions favored the creation of such a social system? To answer this question one must recall that the Romans, who dominated the Mediterranean during the time of Jesus, thought of land as capital, and patronage as sound investment strategy.[29] The ancients, furthermore, lacked what modern industrial societies see as a three-deck structure (lower, middle, upper classes). Ancient Mediterranean society was polarized much more starkly between haves and have-nots, between the privileged few and the disadvantaged many. As a result, social life was not dominated, as ours is, by leading economic indicators, corporate earnings or the gross national product, but by numerous tiny pyramids of power and influence, each headed by a wealthy family whose members acted as patrons to clients of the first, second or third (etc.) order. It is no surprise, therefore, that a great number of records surviving from late antiquity (e.g., Cicero's letters) deal with recommendations for privileges or promotions on behalf of friends (clients).

The patron-client relationship could be either vertical (between unequals) or horizontal (between equals). Further, depending on one's social status or economic class, one might be a patron in one situation and a client in another. A good example of vertical patronage (using the services of a broker) can be seen in the relationship between the Emperor Trajan (the patron), Pliny the Younger (the broker; client to the emperor but patron to others) and Harpocras (the client; Pliny's masseur).[30] Acting as broker/patron for Harpocras (and as client applying for favor from the emperor), Pliny wrote seeking citizen status for his masseur. The emperor (Patron with a capital P) complied.

When the relationship involved equals, it created not permanent hierarchical inequality but reciprocal—and alternating—indebtedness. These debts, however, were not monetary and the bill was paid not in cash sums but in favors returned. Thus, for example, we have records showing that Cicero once provided legal representation for his friend (and social equal) Manius Acilius Glabrio. It would have been socially and morally outrageous for Cicero to send a bill for these services. But later, after Cicero's star had fallen and Glabrio's had risen, the bills began arriving—in the form of favors sought by Cicero on behalf of other friends. Indeed, this whole delicate pattern of mutual backscratching, of shifting patron/client roles among equals, came to be known as *amicitia* (Latin for "friendship"). It referred, of course, not to bonding based on mutual affection but to a delicate dance of debt and obligation that involved an exchange of favors but not of money.[31]

The patronage system was thus one based on notions of moral obligation created by reciprocity. It worked well in a society where the large-scale, bureaucratic institutions that characterize modern nation-states had not yet developed, and where there was no middle class. Under such conditions, power could be concentrated in the hands of a few, and a "dependency ideology" (on the part of the powerless) could be rather easily maintained. Indeed, some scholars view the patron-client structure as essentially integrative and benign—a way of ensuring good political and economic relations between producers and nonproducers. A majority, however, see the system as essentially malevolent and manipulative—a way to perpetuate the power of the elite through conscious cultivation of dependency and vulnerability among the disadvantaged.[32]

Perhaps the best way to summarize what we have discussed about the social world of Jesus' time is to draw up a chart that contrasts contemporary American values and views on a variety of issues (e.g., sense of self, job, friends, relations between men and women) with those of ancient (traditional) Mediterranean culture. The chart provided here has been constructed with the help of data summarized by Bruce Malina and Jerome Neyrey in their intriguing book *Calling Jesus Names: The Social Value of Labels in Matthew*.[33]

While this chart is by no means a complete description of the differences between the ancient Mediterranean world and our own, it may help us understand many things that Jesus' contemporaries took for granted, but which we do not. Slavery, for instance, was acceptable even to good religious folk in Jesus' day—as were radical inequalities between men and women. Today, slavery is regarded as utterly abhorrent, and androcentric sexism can no longer be assumed as the way things ought to be. Unless one understands the kind of world Jesus lived in, with all its assumptions and prejudices, it will be impossible to grasp his message about the need for a radical revolution in human relationships. For as I hope to show in the pages that follow, by offering humanity a new way to experience **69**

U.S. View	Mediterranean View
SENSE OF SELF	
Autonomous, independent; emphasis on individualism and egalitarianism (all are equal)	Heteronomous, dependent on others' view of self; emphasis on hierarchy (patron/client) and other-orientation (honor/shame)
MEN AND WOMEN	
Equal partners in marriage; equal opportunity and equal pay for equal work expected; women and men each make their own decisions; a person-based culture	Wives subject to husbands; women secluded at home—no public role; decisions for women made by others (chiefly, by males); a gender-based culture
FRIENDS	
Friends expected to "be there," to provide emotional support, but usually not material assistance; friends drawn from ranks of both men and women	Friends expected to provide emotional and material help; usually limited to males in the immediate locale (village or neighborhood)
JOB	
Doing job well is paramount; job kept quite distinct from personal life; employers not expected to make allowances for employee's family life or problems; tasks and principles precede relationships and personalities	Being well recognized for doing job is paramount; job and personal life fuse; employer expected to make allowances for employee's family life, circumstances; relationships and personalities precede tasks and determine working principles
THE HOUSEHOLD	
Household duties (cooking, washing, hygiene, eating) are private affairs	Household duties are done in public

OTHERS

Children taught to think of themselves as individuals, first; "fairness" means treating people according to a universal set of rules equally applicable to all; Achievements (especially riches and success) are the individual's; self-respect is all-important

Children taught to think of themselves as "we," as part of group; fairness means treating others according to their rank or social standing; norms are "rank specific"; achievements (success, riches) belong to whole group; Saving face is all-important

AUTHORITY

Submission to other's power and authority is undesirable; power located broadly throughout society; good leaders are consultative, collaborative "team members"

Submission to authority is both desirable and necessary; power is concentrated in the hands of a few; good leaders are paternalistic autocrats

DECISION-MAKING

Belongs to the many; developing consensus is important

Belongs to the few; consensus is not important

NETWORKING

Based on competence, common interests; networks formed from professional contacts

Based on social rank, standing, "connections"; networks consist of friends or "friends of friends"

POLITICS

Rule of law paramount; interests and rights of individuals guaranteed; central government expected to be strong, reliable

Rule of law neither universally accepted nor guaranteed; "rights" based on patronage relationships; weak central government (if one exists at all)

dining, Jesus was inviting us to a new vision of what it means to be human—one that subverted all the old categories of religion, politics and "business as usual."

Banqueting in the Ancient Mediterranean World

The fact that Christians ate together when they assembled as a community is a characteristic they shared in common with virtually every group in the ancient world. Moreover, the same basic patterns and rules of dining were followed whether the meal was designated as a secular or a sacred event. As Dennis Smith and Hal Taussig put it, "On the one hand, there was a religious component to every 'secular' meal. On the other hand every 'sacred' banquet was also a social occasion."[34] For the ancients, dining was dining; the familiar, common traditions that surrounded a meal were present whether the sponsoring group was a trade guild or a religious sect. Any political, religious or ethnic distinctiveness a group of diners might possess was overshadowed by the meal's structure as a social institution that belonged to all members of a given culture.

Certain features, then, routinely characterized all formal meals within the ancient Mediterranean cultural context: posture, location, invitations, furnishings, rankings at table, washings and the proper sequence of courses.

Reclining was the customary posture for formal meals throughout the ancient Mediterranean region, a practice adopted by Greeks, Romans and Jews after the earlier custom (sitting, probably on the ground or on a slightly elevated cushion) had been abandoned. Because it was the space where guests were entertained (recall what was said above about the impact of others' views on self-image and self-esteem), the dining area was often the most elaborately furnished and lavishly decorated room of the house. If the house had no such room—or if the dining area was insufficient for entertaining guests comfortably and properly—banquet facilities for public use (by citizens only) were usually available. Very often these spaces were temples rented out to clients by religious groups who may also have done the food preparation and cooking. Paul, for example, speaks in 1 Corinthians 8 about Christians who attend banquets in such buildings. He notes that it is perfectly all right to eat the food served there (even if it has been sacrificed to idols), though he cautions against doing so if it would compromise those weaker in faith.

Invitations to a festive meal were usually delivered orally, using a standard form. Sometimes the initial invitation was followed by a courtesy reminder. (Note, however, that this system of double invitation presumes that the host is affluent and can easily afford to hire servants/messengers.) The dining room was furnished with couches so the guests could recline. The placing of these couches reflected social ranking, and their arrangement was never left to chance. Etiquette demanded that each guest be placed in proper relation to all the others—a tricky task that often led to embarrassing social gaffes. Ordinarily, the ranking order started at the highest position and continued around the room to the right until the lowest position was reached. It was the custom, too, for diners to share couches; to recline immediately beside the host or guest of honor was to have a privileged position at table.[35] Before reclining, each guest's feet and hands were washed by a household servant. For Jews in Jesus' time, this hand-washing had attained the status of religious ritual.

The proper sequence of an ancient Greco-Roman meal was almost the exact opposite of modern American customs. Among us it is customary to serve cocktails (perhaps with *hors d'oeuvres)* first, followed by the dinner proper (accompanied, in formal contexts, by different wines for the principal courses). In the ancient Mediterranean region, however, this structure is reversed: the (Latin) *cena* or (Greek) *deipnon* (dinner proper, with courses of vegetables and, sometimes, fish or meat) is followed by the (Latin) *convivium* or (Greek) *symposion* (the drinking portion of the event). The ending of the *deipnon* and the beginning of the *symposion* was marked by rather elaborate ritual actions: The tables were removed and the floor swept; water was passed around for washing hands and cups; a wine bowl was brought in for mixing the drinks (usually three parts water to one part wine, or five parts water to two parts wine); the gods were offered a ritual libation (a sometimes complex ceremony involving several mixed bowls and cups of wine); and a hymn or paean was sung. Sometimes perfumes and garlands of flowers were passed among the guests. Among Jews this ritual transition to the *symposion* was marked by a formal *berakah* (blessing): "Blessed are you, Lord our God, King of the universe, Creator of the fruit of the vine!" Such a two-part structure—dinner followed by a drinking party—is clearly assumed in Christian sources such as Luke 22:20 and 1 Corinthians 11:25. Following the ceremonies that introduced the *symposion,* the final course of the whole meal would be served—the so-called "second table" or dessert (usually fruit, nuts and liberal quantities of salt to induce more drinking).

Then, as now, drinking was often linked to entertainment. Party games were popular—such as *kottabos,* a contest to see which drinker could fling the last drops from a nearly empty cup into a wine bowl placed at the center of the dining room.[36] Sometimes the wine-drinking was accompanied by music, dance, drama or acrobatics. Among rowdier types, the *symposion* could become an occasion for other amusements as well, such as erotic liaisons with one's couch-mates, or with the flute girl. (Traditionally, the only women allowed at a *symposion*—at least during the classical era—were entertainers, including musicians who played flute. These women were often treated as little more than prostitutes.)

Among more sober groups (such as religious or philosophical societies), entertainment often took the form of elevated conversation on a given theme. This feature, in fact, appears to have become one of the most important aspects of the *symposion* as it was adapted for use by Jewish and Christian communities. Meals shared by a Jewish sage and his disciples could be characterized by such serious philosophical discussions. And among Christians, almost from the beginning, there are indications that instruction of some kind accompanied the *deipnon/symposion* (see Acts 20:7). Jesus, too, is often portrayed in the gospel traditions as one who teaches while at table (see Luke 14).

The Ideology of Banquets

As anthropologist Mary Douglas has often noted, meals are never simply about food; they are also—and much more fundamentally—about power, strategy and social relations.

> If food is treated as a code, the messages it encodes will be found in the pattern of social relations being expressed. The message is about different degrees of hierarchy, inclusion and exclusion, boundaries and transactions across the boundaries. Like sex, the taking of food has a social component, as well as a biological one.[37]

All meals, then—whether of the ancient Mediterranean or modern varieties—are implicit commentaries on social structure, ranking, hierarchy and power. This pattern of commentary continued even in the historical evolution of specifically religious meals such as the Christian eucharist. Anyone old enough to remember the preconciliar solemn pontifical high Mass will recall that the meal had in fact became an elaborate series of choreographed codes that spoke powerfully about status and rank; inclusion and exclusion (no women were ever allowed "on the altar"); dominance and submission (one bowed, genuflected and knelt before the presiding prelate, kissing all objects handed him for ritual use). The eucharistic meal had become, in fact, a kind of sociological treatise that spoke loudly of gender-based bias (women excluded from active liturgical ministries), marginalization (laity kept "outside the pale," beyond the barrier that separated sanctuary from nave) and **75**

the ideology of caste (a sacred priesthood separate from—
and innately superior to—the profane life of the laity).

I will argue shortly that such an ideology is profoundly
at odds with Jesus' own view of table, meal and ministry.
But for the moment I simply want to note that *all* meals—
including those of Jesus—commit participants to a particular vision of culture and society, while at the same time
engaging them in the symbolic embodiment of what
relations among diners are, can or should be. To participate
in the meal is to enact that vision, to surrender oneself to its
value, meaning and truth. (This seems to have been
precisely the reason why Paul could not go along with
Corinthian meal habits that resulted in polarizing the
community between rich and poor, haves and have-nots,
gluttons and beggars [1 Corinthians 11:17−34]. Recall the
deipnon/symposion structure of ancient meals. Some Corinthian Christians were apparently so eager to "get on with it"
that they took the first places, eating and drinking before all
members of the community could arrive and so creating
divisions of social status, rank and preference in a Body
where all were supposed to be radically *equal.* As a result,
Paul says, it is not the *Lord's* Supper that the Corinthians eat
[1 Corinthians 11:20−21].)

To return to Douglas's point, ancient Greco-Roman
meals (the Christian eucharist among them) represented an
unambiguous code of social relations. They effectively
functioned to define groups and their values, as well as
relations among group members. As ideological devices,
then, these meals created effective bonds, social strata and
ethical obligations among participants. At the level of *social
bonding,* dinner became the primary means of strengthen-
ing and celebrating the diners' identity and solidarity.
Common meals thus became the chief social activity for
members of specific clubs, guilds, associations, philosophical schools or coteries of friends. Indeed, table redefined the
meaning of friendship, bonding participants as a permanent
band with clear membership boundaries.

At the same time, meals clarified a group's *social strata.* Every table in the ancient world was crisscrossed by both visible and invisible boundaries. Reclining, for example, was a posture that in itself indicated social rank. (Because reclining required that one be served, it signaled affluence, membership in a class that could afford to own or hire servants.) Traditionally, this posture was reserved exclusively to males who were also free citizens; it was forbidden to women, children and slaves. In Roman times (the era of Jesus), this older discipline had been somewhat relaxed, however, so that women were sometimes permitted to recline among the men at table. Still, the old gender-based preferences surfaced whenever conflicts arose.

Thus, if a banquet became so crowded that there was no longer any room for a late-arriving male guest, a woman would be expected to yield her spot to the man. (It was considered insulting and "womanish" to *sit* at table; a male latecomer would rather recline on the floor than be caught sitting. It was also considered rude and insensitive for a host to invite too large a gathering to dinner, for this interfered with sociability and good conversation. Thus Plutarch criticized the wealthy who built "showy dining rooms . . . where the manager of a fair is needed more than a toast-master."[38]) Moreover, it was considered ethically appropriate and necessary (a sign of that solidarity and good order which were supposed to characterize a meal among friends) to recognize social status at table. This was done above all by placement, but it could also be accomplished by the quantity and quality of food given to individuals. Occasionally the rules governing social rank might be suspended, as at the Jewish Passover when (according to the Mishnah) even the poorest Israelite should recline at table.[39]

Besides bonding and ranking participants, meals also created a pattern of ethical obligations. These obligations arose not from external laws or rules but from the nature of the bond created among friends around the table. The focus of "table ethics" was always the group as a whole—its unity, happiness, love, pleasure, well-being. Typically, therefore, any behavior that threatens the common good (e.g., quarreling, arguing, abusive remarks) was excluded from table. The table talk had to be such that all present could participate in it without falling into factional rivalries or disputes (hence the warnings Paul gives in 1 Corinthians 11:17–34 and 14:26–33). In a word, *table etiquette became incarnate as ethics* in the ancient Mediterranean ideology of meals. For as Roland Barthes once said,

> To eat is a behavior that develops beyond its own ends, replacing, summing up, and signaling other behaviors. . . . Today, we might say all of them: activity, work, sports, effort, leisure, celebration—every one of these situations is expressed through food.[40]

We may thus summarize the multiple meanings implied by the ancient world's ideology of meals and table-sharing by noting, with Lee Edward Klosinski, that

> eating together is far more than the ingestion of comestibles. It can symbolize a complex number of feelings and relationships, mediate social status and power, and be a means of expressing the boundaries of group identity. . . . Sharing food is a transaction which involves a series of mutual obligations and which initiates an interconnected complex of mutuality and reciprocity. . . . [We may also note] *the ability of food to symbolize these relationships.* . . .
>
> Food exchanges are basic to human interaction. Implicit in them is a series of obligations to give, receive and repay. . . .
>
> In Greco-Roman antiquity food and commensality [table-sharing] also functioned as mechanisms for social formation and organization.[41]

Jesus and the Table

As I noted earlier in this chapter, it is no longer plausible to think of Jesus and his earliest companions as a bunch of country bumpkins who couldn't tell a baked squash from a roast leg of lamb. They were well aware of the way meals functioned both within Jewish family life and within the larger context of hellenized Mediterranean culture. They understood the table's power to include or exclude, to create debts and obligations, to symbolize dominance and power. In short, they understood that to change dining habits was, quite literally, to change the world. For at table, everything that creates the world is present: economics, politics, power, the potential for rivalry and competition, bonds among friends, boundaries against enemies. In the following pages, I will try to show how Jesus' table ministry was, in fact, a strategy for rebuilding human community on principles radically different from those of his surrounding social and religious culture—different from the ideology of honor and shame, of patrons, clients and brokers, of "us" against "them." And I will suggest that a similar strategy for re-creating human community under-girds the process that leads from water-bath to eucharistic dining in the assembly of believers.

As John Dominic Crossan has so skillfully shown, Jesus

> negated alike and at once the hierarchical and patronal nor-malcies of Jewish religion and Roman power. . . . He was neither broker nor mediator but, somewhat paradoxically, the announcer that neither should exist between humanity and divinity or between humanity and itself.[42]

God is *always* arriving in the world, is *already* given over to people. God chooses relatedness to us as the sole definition of the Divine, and so has "disappeared" into humanity and can be found "nowhere else but there."[43] The relation between God and humans, Jesus thus announced, no longer needs to be mediated or brokered—but simply celebrated as a *fait accompli,* a done deed. The celebration begins at a table where all are equal and continues in lives lived wholly as justice and mercy.

The radical character of Jesus' unbrokered and table-centered vision of relations between God and world, person and person, unfolded in several strategies, four of which will occupy our attention here. The first of these was Jesus' repudiation of existing social and religious systems. The second was his practice of "radical itinerancy" (or what, today, we might more commonly call "vagrancy," "homelessness"). The third was his reputation as a healer of battered humans. And the fourth was his controversial custom of table-companionship with the unexpected, the unworthy and the unlikely.

Protest The world of Jesus' day (like our own) was one in which there were great opportunities for wealth as well as for oppression. (This is typical of societies polarized between the very affluent and the very poor—with a dwindling or nonexistent middle class.) In major cities of the Roman empire, such as Sepphoris, the provincial capital of Galilee, the deliberate embracing of poverty—voluntary "grunginess"—was a popular form of social protest against the excesses of "yuppiedom." Among the greatest proponents of such protest were the Cynics, a philosophical group that challenged the civilized virtues of Greco-Roman life by emphasizing countercultural values of radical simplicity, spontaneity and naturalness, freedom and egalitarianism.

The Cynics' way of life—especially their choices of food, dress and shelter—made them both very visible and very annoying to their wealthier contemporaries. As Leif Vaage has described them,

> The standard uniform of the Cynics was a cloak, a wallet [more like our modern backpack], a staff. Typically, their life included barefooted itinerancy, viz., indigence, sleeping on the ground or in the baths and other public buildings, a diet of water and vegetables. They were found usually in the market-place. They begged.[44]

Add to this long hair and a long beard, and you have the picture of a person who is not likely to win approval from the better class of Roman citizenry. Quite deliberately, it seems, the Cynics sought freedom from convention (in matters of dwelling, food and apparel) as a key to liberating themselves from that system of desires (based on ideologies of honor and shame; on patrons, brokers and clients) which enthralled Greco-Roman civilization. They formed an "army of the dog," whose opponents accused them of stupidity, shamelessness, debauchery, beggary and theft.[45]

It is certainly possible that Jesus and his companions reflected a kind of Jewish-peasant version of this Cynical contempt for the specious values championed by the upwardly mobile members of Mediterranean society. Like the Cynic "grungies," the Jesus group appears to have developed an unenviable and smelly reputation for irregularity in matters of behavior, attitude, associations and priorities. They appear to have repudiated the whole social system of patrons and clients as simply a way to institutionalize inequality and to systematize oppression. Similarly, on the level of religious belief and practice, they appear to have rejected a brokered relationship with God. For Jesus, it was not so much that Temple and priesthood are wicked and wrong; they are simply irrelevant. Perhaps that is why the New Testament writers recorded stories of Jesus' symbolically "destroying" the Temple (see Mark 11:15–16 and parallels). He did this by bringing its fiscal, sacrificial and liturgical operations to a screeching halt. This "cleansing" of a sacred religious site was a classic Cynic's deed, for the Temple was the seat of everything non-egalitarian, patriarchal, patronal and oppressive within Jewish political and religious life.[46]

But the Temple was not the only institution Jesus criticized. He saved some of his most acerbic barbs for that icon of late twentieth-century religious-right rhetoric, the *family*. To the surprise and bewilderment of many readers, the New Testament contains some very hostile comments about Jesus' relatives. They regarded him as a loose cannon, a lunatic who should be kept out of public view (Mark 3:20–21). Relations were apparently so strained at one point that Jesus refused to meet with "his mother, brothers and sisters" (Mark 3:31–35), preferring instead to stay close

81

to his "new family" of like-minded companions. As the evangelists remember him, Jesus was thus quite critical of the family system of his day, probably because it depended for its survival upon patriarchy and privilege—upon a system of "superiors" and "inferiors," "greater ones" and "lesser ones," rather than upon the coequal integrity and value of each member.

The institution of marriage, too, was the object of Jesus' scrutiny and critique. Much ink has been spilled over Jesus' saying in Mark 10:11, "Whoever divorces his wife and marries another commits adultery against her." Most Catholic commentators have seen in this text a general prohibition against divorce (and by implication a defense of the "indissoluble bond" of matrimony). But this interpretation misses the point. In Jesus' day, no one would really have cared about any alleged (or real) injury to a woman caused by divorce. "Honor" and "shame" were androcentric prerogatives—only the male's rights and injuries were considered legally or socially important.

Two things about Jesus' comment are startling. First, he insists that a woman's honor has as much right to be defended as a man's. Second, he implies that, even so, "honor" is a sham commodity, a false virtue—and that the real source of destruction, in marriage as in other intimate relations, is an androcentric bias that dehumanizes women, denies their vulnerability, and defends their ill treatment by appealing to an ideology of "saving face." The whole patriarchal system of human relations—and not just those of marriage—is thus called into question.

Vagrancy It was bad enough that Jesus wore the wrong clothes, ate the wrong food and hung out with the wrong crowd. Worse, he had a bad attitude. Worse still, he liked living as a vagrant, wandering and homeless. Such a life (then as now!) placed a person in one of three categories: The homeless one is either a "mental case" (e.g., an alcoholic schizophrenic), an irresponsible, lazy and shiftless "bum" (unwilling to work or unable to hold a steady job) or an outlaw (who survives by preying upon others). All these accusations appear to have been made against Jesus. His family thought he was crazy; religious opponents saw him as a shiftless troublemaker who sucked up to sinners and tax collectors (toadies representing the oppressive Roman bureaucracy); still others perceived him as a degenerate deviant who lived like an outlaw, fleeing from house to house and town to town.

Above all, of course, vagrants are dirty, literally and figuratively. Dirt, as Mary Douglas has noted, is "matter out of place . . . in some undesired way."[47] It threatens all whom it touches with disarray, disorder. When the dirt is attached to a person, it signals deviance, a violation of assumed expectations and rules of conduct. Hence the phenomenon, in virtually all cultures, of labeling, of name-calling. As Bruce Malina and Jerome Neyrey note,

> To label a person or group negatively is a social act of retaliation for some alleged deviance. Under certain circumstances . . . such labeling is (1) a serious challenge to honor . . . (2) an unprovoked act of aggression . . . or (3) an act of assault. . . . New Testament epithets such as "sinner," "unclean," "demon-possessed" and "brood of vipers," much like epithets in our society such as "whore," "ex-con," "Commie," "quack," "pervert" and the like, are not simply vaporous words. *They are social weapons.* In the hands of influential persons or powerful groups, they can inflict genuine injury, since they serve to define a person as permanently out of social place, hence as permanently deviant. . . . In a society built on grades of status [such as the Mediterranean culture of Jesus' day], degrading terms that stick almost necessarily lead to collective avoidance, ostracism and isolation.[48]

Jesus and his followers appear to have adopted vagrancy as the way of life that best embodied their vision of a new society based on unbrokered egalitarianism. Instead of settling down in one spot, hiring an agent, buying air time (or better still, a network) and marketing himself as a spiritual broker, Jesus found "nowhere to lay his head," and prayed for food and forgiveness one day at a time. Jesus refused to make himself an industry. Instead of relying on well-heeled patrons, powerful family patriarchs, or influential friends of friends—staples of ancient Mediterranean culture—Jesus and his disciples had to start anew every morning.

In a word, Jesus and his circle did not engage in a slick, self-sufficient mission that would make others dependent upon them. Self-sufficiency would have transformed their healing ministry into an institutionalized, charitable program that places the healed in a subordinate relation of indebtedness to their healers. So Jesus and his companions traveled with the barest minimum of dress and equipment: no extra clothing, no cash reserves, no surplus supplies of food and drink. They entrusted themselves and their daily needs to the hospitality and openness of others. *The relation between healer and healed thus became one of complete mutuality, reciprocity.* Each depended upon the other for something vital; there were no classes of "givers" and "takers," no (independent) philanthropists *versus* (dependent) "clients."

Healing   By living as a vagrant and an "outlaw," Jesus avoided the trap of brokered dependency into which professional healers usually fall. (Nothing is worse than being dependent on the virtuous. Ask anyone who has ever lived with a saint!) Jesus recognized that the sick and battered—indeed, *all* those who need healing—also have gifts of inestimable value to give to their thealers. He thus redefined the relationship established in the act of healing— making it one of complete reciprocity, where blessings are bestowed from *both* sides.

But there is more. Jesus also denied the connection many of his contemporaries made between sickness and sin. Recall the gospel story of the man born blind (John 9; a text used each year on the Fourth Sunday of Lent in parishes where the initiation process is in place and candidates are being readied for initiation at Easter). In that story, the first question asked by Jesus' uncomprehending disciples is "Who sinned, this man or his parents, that he was born blind?" Their assumption, of course, is that physical affliction or illness is a sure sign of moral failure. Jesus, however, disputes this assumption by flatly asserting that neither the blind son nor his parents are guilty of any sin (John 9:3).

For Jesus, then, sickness and disability are neither symptoms of sin, nor symbols of divine displeasure, nor retribution for immoral conduct. In adopting such a view, he decisively rejected the familiar human habit of blaming the victim. As John Dominic Crossan notes, such a rejection was utterly revolutionary:

> There is . . . a terrible irony in [the] conjunction of sickness and sin, especially in first-century Palestine. Excessive taxation could leave poor people physically malnourished or hysterically disabled. But *since the religiopolitical ascendancy could not blame excessive taxation, it blamed sick people themselves by claiming that their sins had led to their illnesses.* And the cure for sinful sickness was, ultimately, in the Temple. And that meant more fees, in a perfect circle of victimization. *When, therefore, . . . Jesus with a magical touch cured people of their sicknesses, [he] implicitly declared their sins forgiven or nonexistent.* [Jesus] challenged not the medical monopoly of the doctors but the religious monopoly of the priests. All this was religiopolitically subversive.[49]

The implications of Jesus' view were enormous. It shattered the vicious cycle of victimization followed by blaming the victim, and simultaneously subverted the cultic industry that had grown up around the (illegitimate) connection between sickness and sin. Moreover, by refusing to make himself a "professional" or his healings a "business," Jesus removed sickness from the patron-broker-client system. (Recall the story of the healing of Peter's mother-in-law [Mark 1:29 ff.]. As word of Jesus' power to cure spread, the sick and their families began crowding around Peter's door. It would have been a perfect opportunity for opening a cottage clinic, with Peter acting as broker between Jesus and the clients seeking help. Instead,

Jesus moves on, refuses to settle in a single location, rejects the temptation to turn curative powers into healing for hire.)

Jesus thus responded to sickness not as a religious professional but as a human being who shared, simply and immediately, the hunger of those he healed. *Touching* was his characteristic mode of response. "Moved with pity, he stretched out his hand [to the leper] and *touched* him" (Mark 1:41); "He *touched* her hand, and the fever left her" (Matthew 8:15); "He *touched* their eyes and said 'Let it be done for you according to your faith'" (Matthew 9:29); "He *touched* the servant's ear and healed him" (Luke 22:51); "The woman said, 'If only I can *touch* his cloak, I will be cured'" (Matthew 9:21); "People brought to him all those who were sick . . . that they might *touch* only the tassel on his cloak, and as many as *touched* it were healed" (Matthew 14:35–36). By touching, Jesus not only signaled solidarity with the sick, he actually participated in their uncleanness, in their ostracism and opprobrium—experiencing with them the disgust and judgmental superiority of those "righteous ones" who make a business of blaming victims.

All this has been beautifully summarized by George Hunsinger in an essay on "Jesus and the Leper":

> When we see Jesus reaching out to the leper, when we see him touching the untouchable, when we see him assuming the leper's defilement and becoming as a leper himself, what we are witnessing is an event laden with the mystery of the atonement. For in this act of compassion—whereby the leper is cleansed but only as Jesus is made unclean—we may catch a glimpse of how Jesus changes place with us.[50]

Moreover, as Jesus himself was an "outlaw," a prophet who lived and died "outside the camp," so those who are healed by him must forever remain "outsiders":

> Those who have been touched by Jesus . . . and healed are not expected to be respectable or conventional. They are expected to be outside the camp. They are expected to work for peace . . . when the world seems hell-bent on . . . destruction, and for the integrity of creation at a time of its increasing

desecration. They are expected to cry out against the injustice visited upon the world's vast majority who are poor, hungry and oppressed. They are expected to stand up for those who are systematically abused and excluded merely because of their gender or sexual orientation. They are expected to know that "God stands at every time on this and only on this side: always against the exalted and for the lowly, always against those who already have rights and for those from whom they are robbed and taken away" (Karl Barth).[51]

As a healer, then, Jesus severed the connection between sickness and sin, subverted the brokered system of cultic cleansings that makes money from victims' distress, and repudiated the religious professionalism that renders compassion a "work for hire."

Table   If we ask, then, what the original movement begun by Jesus and his first followers was like, we could say that it was aimed primarily at the rural population (in the countryside and small villages) rather than at residents of large urban centers; that it reflected a "Jewish peasant Cynicism" rather than a Greco-Roman one; that it was "populist/grass roots" rather than "professional/religious"; that it repudiated exclusionary social and religious systems based on brokered patron/client relations or honor/shame ideologies; that it promoted a radical egalitarianism in which women were full and equal partners with men. Jesus thus stressed the openness and obviousness of his message: "You have eyes and ears, use them!" God's reign is not cryptic and hidden, requiring religious experts to discern its presence; it's as obvious as blowing wind or waving corn (hence available to anyone who observes nature's mysteries). God's reign is about the inborn worth and value of persons, not about authorities and hierarchies. (What if one sheep really *is* as valuable as ninety-nine? What then?)

Because our bodies are microcosms of the social body (and vice versa), the oppression of the many by the few equals "possession" (control of the weak by the strong).   **87**

Hence Jesus acts as an exorcist, liberating persons from bondage to powerful oppressors, human or inhuman. Because in the world of Galilean peasants a child is a nobody, "the reign of God is like children" (i.e., it is "a kingdom of nobodies"; Matthew 19:14). Because in a world of Roman oppression, upward mobility is restricted to those who already have, the reign of God belongs to the *ptochoi,* the destitute, the undesirables, not the respectable poor. Because in a world of tightly controlled, centralized religion, God's blessing is thought to belong to the pure and upright, the reign of God appears smelly and corrupt (like leaven), priceless but useless (like a pearl), embarrassing (What if you gave a dinner and all the invited guests stood you up?) and unjust (What if somebody hired at the last minute gets the same wages as the person who's worked all day?).

Jesus' career as peasant protester, outlaw, vagrant and healer continued in "commensality" (the shared companionship of table). In this connection, it is important to recognize that he carried out his ministry not only as "one who *gives*" but as "one who *receives.*" Perhaps that is why the gospels remember such curious details as the "dress-and-equipment codes" of the Jesus group. According to Matthew 10:9–10, those who collaborate with Jesus in his mission are forbidden to carry money, bags, extra clothing ("two tunics"), sandals or staffs. Why? Because those necessities would have made them self-sufficient professionals with their own means and resources. And such independent professionals (however devout their intentions and motives may be) always end up assuming positions of power, patronage, brokerage—precisely the socio-religious system Jesus found oppressive, destructive and repugnant. For Jesus, it was crucial that the members of his mission be *needy,* that they be receivers and not just givers. What he and his disciples had to offer was a miracle (healing) and a message (the reign of God is already arriving, already active and present among you). What they had to receive, in return, was "a table and a house."[52]

That is why, in Jesus' view, table sharing is not almsgiving. Almsgiving is *power* giving to *need*. It does not alter the basic social situation (power and goods concentrated in the hands of a few) nor does it make people truly equal. "Generous almsgiving may even be conscience's last great refuge against the terror of open commensality."[53] What Jesus had in mind was not such charity, but a shared egalitarianism of spiritual and material resources where each person at table served, simultaneously, as giver and receiver, as host and guest, as nourisher and nourished, as need and plenty, as hunger and food. Jesus comes to the table not as patron, presider or professional, but as needy stranger who has traveled a long way without money, food, footgear or a change of clothing. Jesus comes to the table not offering hospitality but *needing* it.

Eucharist: The Table of the Needy

This, then, was one of the most scandalous aspects of Jesus' message, method and mission. He sat at table not as the charming, congenial, ringleted centerpiece of a Rembrandt painting, but as a vulnerable vagrant willing to share potluck with a household of strangers. Normally, a table's prime function is to establish social ranking and hierarchy (by what one eats, how one eats, with whom one eats). Normally, a meal is about social identification, status and power. (We don't call them "power lunches" for nothing!) But the very *randomness* of Jesus' table habits challenged this system of social relations modeled on meals and manners.

It wasn't simply that Jesus ate with objectionable persons —outcasts and sinners—but that he ate with anyone, indiscriminately. Hence his reputation: He has no honor! He has no shame! As Crossan shows, Jesus' strategy of table sharing was not simply a way to support himself "on the cheap," nor even a way to symbolize, dramatically, his vision of God's reign. Rather, commensality was "a strategy for building or rebuilding peasant community on radically different principles from those of honor and shame, patronage and clientage."[54] For Jesus, *healing* (the gift he brings to a home) calls forth *hospitality* (those healed offer refreshment, food and drink, a place at table).

The table companionship practiced by Jesus thus re-created the world, redrew all of society's maps and flow charts. Instead of symbolizing social rank and order, it blurred the distinctions between hosts and guests, need and plenty. Instead of reinforcing rules of etiquette, it subverted them, making the last first and the first last. In Christian tradition, of course, the collective name given to the behaviors and actions of Jesus and his companions at table is "eucharist." Too often, however, we have framed our understanding of Jesus' eucharistic teaching and practice by focusing exclusively on the New Testament's reports of a *Last* Supper, a farewell meal shared by Jesus and his friends. Whatever the importance, facts and drama surrounding this Supper may have been, it does not account for Jesus' reputation as a "regular" at strangers' tables, a "glutton and drunkard" who eats with sinners—a reputation that made him a very problematic figure not only for his enemies but also for his friends. In what follows, I shall try to trace *Jesus'* understanding and practice of eucharistic dining—as distinct from the myriad ways later generations of Christians took over this tradition, adapting it in their own time, altering it for their own purposes.

Great Supper, Not "Last Supper"   I have already drawn attention to the fact that Jesus scandalized family, friends and enemies by the company he kept. His contemporaries were bothered not just by the sort of people he hung out with (e.g., those marginalized by "the moral majority," by poverty, social oppression, gender or sexual stigma), but by the fact that he reclined at table anywhere, with anyone. Why should this cause such intense and hostile reactions?

Perhaps the question can best be answered by looking for the foundations of Jesus' eucharistic teaching *not* in the Last Supper narratives but in the Great Supper parable, which appears in the New Testament gospels of Luke (14:16–24) and Matthew (22:1–14) and in the noncanonical Gospel of Thomas (#64). As this popular story circulated in early Christian communities, it was shaped by pastoral and polemical concerns about who were the "really true and faithful disciples" of Jesus. Each of our sources addresses this concern from its own special viewpoint.

For the community of the Gospel of Thomas, it is not those deeply entangled in the world's commerce and affairs (businessmen, merchants) who will feast in God's kingdom; rather, as the larger context of the story in Thomas shows, it is the other-worldly celibates and ascetics who will taste the Great Supper of God.

For Luke, those who have arrogantly refused God's feast are the "privileged religious professionals" (Pharisees, scribes); in their place, the suffering outcasts of Israel (the poor, maimed, blind and lame) will be invited first—to be followed by devout and believing Gentiles (those in "the highways and hedges"; Luke 14:23).

Finally, Matthew has upped the ante of the story considerably: The host is now a monarch; the dinner, a marriage feast; the original invitees react in a pattern of escalating abuse and violence; the latter invitees are "both good and bad"; and one unfortunate latecomer, who has no wedding garment, is summarily cast out of the banquet hall. For Matthew, there are—ominously—enemies within the fold, and not until God's final judgment will the chaff be separated from the wheat.

Despite these many variations, certain structural elements of the Great Supper story are steady: A host plans a dinner, issues invitations, is spurned by the original invitees and opens the dining room to "replacement" guests. When

91

placed in the larger context of Jesus' teaching about food, table and culture, this story makes a crucial contribution to eucharistic doctrine.

First, Food Jesus had already argued that food taboos have no meaning or merit—that one cannot use food to evaluate a person's moral integrity or religious devotion. "Whatever enters a person from outside cannot defile . . . but what comes out of a person, that is what defiles" (Mark 7:18–20; cf. 7:15–16). This was already a radical departure from the world of domination and control. For food is not only something we eat, it is our fundamental means of controlling people, of gauging their social standing (the rich do not usually eat pickled pigs' feet or red beans and rice), and, often, of determining their religious allegiance (cf. the Jewish prohibition against pork products). By declaring all foods clean, Jesus "decreed" that the natural bounty of the world (its animal and vegetable produce) may no longer legitimately be used to hold the hungry hostage or to engineer perverse systems of social control and oppression.

Second, Table Jesus relativized the role of table rituals. Knowledge and practice of them is no longer a relevant criterion for assessing a person's human worth, cultural condition or religious reputability. The rituals of washing hands, of purifying pots, bowls and utensils, are dismissed by Jesus not as evil but simply as irrelevant and superfluous (see Mark 7:1–15). This meant, of course, that one is free to associate at table with those who do not know such rituals (i.e., with the culturally and religiously "unclean").

Third, Cooking and Culture Most cultures distinguish certain foods as quintessentially human and dismiss others as unfit for consumption, uncivilized, on the principle that just because an item is edible doesn't mean it should be eaten. In a word, a culture often underscores its distinctiveness (its difference from all other cultures) by means of its culinary repertoire—and not only by what it eats, but by the way it prepares and serves those foods. That is why the "great cuisines" of the world (Chinese, French, Italian, for example) are instantly identifiable, even when they make use of the same fruits, vegetables, meats and fish. Moreover, a culture's sense of self—its ways of creating meaningful division in time and space—are intimately linked to its cooking habits. Thus certain foods, prepared in certain ways, become, by their presence or absence, symbols of that culture's self-definition (e.g., the chicken or roast beef as an essential part of Sunday dinner; the absence of meat on certain days of penance). Jesus, however, seems to have disputed the value of all such culinary strategies and symbol systems—from the simplest (the basic distinction between raw food and cooked) to the most sacred (the setting aside of certain foods for strictly religious purposes). Thus his disciples snack on raw food, picked at forbidden times, on the principle that even sacred food dedicated to God alone can be eaten if humans need it (see Luke 6:1–5).

In sum, Jesus declared that food, table rites and cooking customs can no longer be used as foundations for a religious or cultural system that is restrictive and exclusionary. The paradoxical conclusion of the Great Supper parable is that all limits are off-limits. *Anyone* may eat *anything* with *anybody* at *any time*. There are no more fences around the table. As Crossan writes,

> It is that "anyone" that negates the very social function of table, namely, to establish a social ranking by what one eats, how one eats, and with whom one eats. It is the random and open commensality of the parable's meal that is its most startling element. One could, in such a situation, have classes, sexes, ranks, and grades all mixed up together. The social challenge of such egalitarian commensality is the radical threat of the parable's vision. It is only a story, of course, but it is one that

focuses its egalitarian challenge on society's mesocosmic mirror, the table as the place where bodies meet to eat. . . .

Open commensality profoundly negates distinctions and hierarchies between female and male, poor and rich, Gentile and Jew. It does so, indeed, at a level that would offend the ritual laws of any civilized society. That was precisely its challenge.[55]

A Meal Without Autocrats What Jesus proposed, then, was a meal in which unconditional acceptance (anyone!) and mutual service (the ability to give *and* receive) outweigh all other cultural or religious considerations. Such a view distinguishes the eucharistic teaching of Jesus from virtually every other parallel in the ancient world. Among the Essenes at Qumran near the Dead Sea, for example, meals were certainly an important feature of community life—but they were dominated by an emphasis on hierarchy, precedence and degrees of dignity:

> When they gather for the common table, to eat and to drink new wine . . . let no man extend his hand over the first-fruits of bread and wine before the Priest; for . . . he shall be the first to extend his hand over the bread. Thereafter, the Messiah of Israel shall extend his hand over the bread, and all the congregation of the community shall utter a blessing, each man in the order of his dignity.[56]

The Essenes are clearly a community "hierarchically assembled." The parallelism between food rules and religious rank remains intact. Distinctions among sacred foods and sacred functions are still very much in place. How different a picture it is, however, when one looks at the accounts of Jesus' table actions in the New Testament (even though these accounts already show signs of a ritualizing trend among early Christians). There is, first, the shocking passage in John's gospel, chapter 13, where the words of Jesus at the supper (a very early tradition already known and quoted by Paul in 1 Corinthians 11:23–26) are replaced by the deed of foot-washing. Such a deed of course destroys all semblance of social rank and hierarchy at the table—for what can such distinctions mean when the guest of honor grovels like a servant? Similarly, Peter's objections ("You will never wash my feet!") are dismissed as *culture* talking—as Jesus explains that learning to *receive* hospitality is as important as learning to give it.

But more startling still are those four words Mark uses to describe Jesus' actions at the farewell meal with his friends: He *took, blessed, broke, gave.* The verbal pattern indicates, first, that whatever food is available is distributed alike to all (even to the traitor at table!). There is no attempt to establish a hierarchy of favorites on the basis of who gets what to eat. (Nor, significantly, does Mark's account contain a command to repeat Jesus' Last Supper deeds as any kind of memorial—though such a tradition was already known to Paul.) Further, the pattern suggests a disturbing incongruity. For of the four words, one pair belongs to the world of masters and autocrats (taking, blessing) while the other pair belongs to the world of servants and scullery maids (breaking, giving). Recall that in the ancient world, the posture of reclining at table—itself a symbol of social distinction and rank—required that diners be *served.* In the experience of most of Jesus' first followers, such service would very likely have been performed not by (male) slaves, but by *women.* Preparing food—and/or serving it at table—were gender-linked activities, women's work. So in the astonishing scene painted by Mark, Jesus takes on the role not only of servant but of female:

> Not only servile but female hosting is symbolized by those four verbs. Far from reclining and being served, *Jesus himself serves the meal, serves, like any housewife, the same meal to all including himself.* Later, of course . . . it would happen that just as the female both serves food and becomes food, so Jesus would both have served food here below and would become food hereafter. . . . *But long before Jesus was host, he was hostess.*[57]

One final point should be noted here. Not only, in Mark's view, are there no autocrats at the Lord's Last Supper; not only is the same food distributed to all alike, without distinction; but *all twelve disciples drink from the same cup.* As Lee Klosinksi has shown, there is bitter irony in this innocent scene of cup-sharing, for it is connected with Mark's conviction that *all twelve are party to Jesus' betrayal.*[58] Ironically, those who share equal dignity at the table also share equal responsibility for failure, and will share equally in the cross ("cup" is Marcan code for both Jesus' and the community's passion and suffering). For Mark, the table is truly and totally egalitarian: It signals not only the end of all autocracies, it also signals that the life and death of *each* is inextricably bound to the life and death of *all.*

"Do This in Memory of Me"   Although Mark's gospel (and Matthew's) contains no command of Jesus to repeat his actions at the Supper, other New Testament sources do (Paul, Luke). We may well ask, however, just *what* it is that we are commanded to repeat in 1 Corinthians 11:24–25 and Luke 22:19. Because we usually assume that the Last Supper served as the root of all later eucharistic ritual, we also assume that the command to repeat means reenacting Jesus' gestures of taking, blessing, breaking and giving. But this is not quite as simple as it sounds. For one thing (as we have seen), these four verbs actually embrace two very different modes of action; they require us to think of the meal in radically egalitarian terms, and to think of Jesus as both host and hostess. (Is the command to repeat properly fulfilled, for instance, in a celebration where hierarchical distinctions of rank and status are signified by voice, vesture, posture, precedence and restricted access to bread and cup?)

For another thing, in some parts of the New Testament —above all in Mark's gospel—the Last Supper, far from being a beautiful story about Jesus' instituting the eucharist, is in fact a scandalous tale of incomprehension and betrayal. It is "the last of many meals in which the disciples have failed to grasp the significance of Jesus and his ministry."[59]

For Mark, the scene at the supper is not so much a sacramental event as a final proof of failure that reaches its climax when one of the disciples' own number becomes Jesus' betrayer. "The scandal of Mark's Last Supper narrative," writes Robert Fowler, "is that Jesus' own disciples will abandon him and one will even deliver him up."[60] Shocking as it may seem, it is quite possible that Mark's Last Supper scene was written not so much to commemorate eucharistic origins as to criticize those Christians whose ritual meals failed to reflect Jesus' revolutionary emphasis on egalitarianism and inclusivity. For Mark, ironically, the (male!) disciples are not faithful custodians of a eucharistic tradition but blind and inept bunglers whose obtuseness leads to their master's apprehension by his enemies.[61]

Do *what,* then, in memory of Jesus? Certainly the church's eventual answer to this question was "celebrate the eucharist." But arriving at this answer took some time — and in the process, some important pieces of the puzzle may have gotten lost. It is my conviction that our understanding of the eucharist is significantly enriched if we take the time to recover a fuller sense of what the New Testament tells us, directly or by implication, about the meals Jesus shared with others.

Culture As we've already seen, the cultural context of Jesus' time already provided a natural focus for a community's relationships, boundaries and social identity: the formal meal consisting, in Greco-Roman times, of the two-part *deipnon* (dinner) and *symposion* (drinking party). This kind of dining was known and practiced throughout the ancient Mediterranean world by Gentiles and Jews alike. As Dennis Smith has said,

> Meals in the setting of a private home, a philosophical gathering, a sacrifice, a club, or a Christian assembly did not differ in their forms so much as they differed in the interpretations given to those forms according to the contexts in which the meals took place.[62]

Thus the first and most obvious meaning of "Do this in memory of me" is *"Assemble for a meal.* Do what humans in our culture usually do when they want to enjoy one another's companionship: Gather as bodies around a table."

Multiple Meanings   One of the fascinating features about Jesus' meals is the broad variety of their contexts and the multiplicity of their meanings. As Dennis Smith points out in an engrossing essay on table fellowship in Luke's gospel,

> Sometimes Jesus is presented as host of the meal, sometimes as guest, sometimes as servant. Sometimes he dines with the righteous (Pharisees), sometimes with "sinners," sometimes with the "crowd" (Luke 9:16). Similarly, sometimes the reader is to see himself or herself as guest (e.g., 5:27–32), sometimes as host (e.g., 14:12–14), sometimes as servant (e.g., 12:42–46; 22:24–27).[63]

To attempt to develop a complete eucharistic understanding from the Last Supper accounts alone would represent a terrible diminishment of our New Testament sources. Jesus' farewell meal was, after all, the last of a (presumably) long series—and hence its meaning is cumulative, embracing the whole history of friends dining together.

A second meaning of "Do this in memory of me" is thus *"Gather up all your fleshly memories of table*—of food and fun, tears and laughter, mellowness and mirth—for they have become your own body. Your body is both *at* the table and *on* the table. You are looking at what you have become."

Freedom from Bondage   In the ancient world, every formal meal was both a blessing and a curse. On the one hand, it was a chance to partake of nature's bounty and to share it with others; on the other, the requirements surrounding social rank could make "seating" (actually, reclining) a very delicate and nerve-racking business. The dining room resembled a minefield: A bit too much of this or too little of that could ruin the whole occasion and cause lasting loss of face and social standing. As we have seen, Jesus' strategy was thus to release the whole ensemble of food/table rites/culinary customs from their bondage to cultural convention (a system of brokered relations that institutionalizes inequality and dependency) and to religious regulation (a system that supports hierarchical control of "holiness"). In place of a commensality that emphasized rank, status, obligation and control, Jesus practiced a subversively *open commensality* that meant one could eat anything with anyone at any time. In place of "perfect adherence to the law," Jesus transgressed rules that were unresponsive to human need (he ate with sinners—Mark 2:15; he and his disciples picked grain on the sabbath—Mark 2:23).

A third meaning of "Do this in memory of me" is thus *"Free yourselves from the compulsion to control persons, places and events.* Free yourselves from bondage to rules that ignore human need. Break your bread gladly with any and all—leaving to God the task of distinguishing the worthy from the unworthy (for many of us who try to strain gnats swallow camels!) Know that God is often feted in the guise of a stranger (Hebrews 13:2; Genesis 18:1–15), and that *receiving* hospitality is as great a grace as giving it."

A Table Where All Can Meet   Many of the practices and beliefs we modern Christians take for granted were not so obvious to the earliest generations of believers. Among these was the ticklish question of whether Jewish and Gentile Christians could sit down together at the same table. (For many Jews, eating with Gentiles would have meant breaking God's law and becoming unclean.) Was eucharistic dining destined to be a *barrier* separating persons along racial and ethnic lines, or would it become a *bridge* bringing them together? Underlying this question were even more basic questions: Should the Christian community be a closed one, or one that is multicultural, multiethnic and racially diverse? Are the disciples of Jesus radically exclusive or inclusive?

99

Christians such as the evangelist Mark came down strongly on the side of *inclusivity,* and they structured their reports of Jesus' meals to support this point of view. In so doing, Mark redefined discipleship and holiness in terms of food. Becoming a disciple, participating in the new kind of holiness envisioned by Jesus, meant taking part in an inclusive table fellowship. It entailed a revolutionary (and highly controversial) understanding of social status and hierarchy. It meant associating with—and offering the reign (presence) of God to—persons who, by the normal standards of Judaism, were wicked.[64] The primary personal and social virtue sought among the members of this newly emergent, culturally/racially/ethnically diversified community was to be *diakonia,* service at table, the work of a slave:

> The necessity of performing this type of service is incumbent upon all members of the community (Mark 10:44–45). In a world where social status was characterized by verticality, *diakoneo* subverts the categories of power, prestige, and rank. Whereas in antiquity people joined associations to carve out a niche of status and recognition for themselves, the appeal of the Marcan community's table fellowship was the possibility of a more egalitarian context . . . in which *one's rank could be measured by one's capacity to serve. The fact that the gospel holds out faithful women who served Jesus as paradigms of true discipleship supports this view.*[65]

A fourth meaning of "Do this in memory of me" is this: *"Your table must be as inclusive as God's mercy.* It must embrace the sinner, the 'morally irregular,' the 'ritually unclean.' *It must welcome precisely those for whom there is no room at any other table."*

An Abundant Table   As scholars like Robert Fowler have pointed out, it is important (though contrary to common practice) to read the Last Supper accounts in light of Jesus' earlier meals with friends and foes, and not vice versa. Not only were those meals characterized by openness and inclusivity, some of them also were remembered as moments of miraculous abundance (see Mark 6:34–44; 8:1–9). Perhaps that is why early Christian tradition (as represented by Mark's gospel, at any rate) contains so many references to eating, drinking, cups, loaves, banquets, feasts, foods, fasting, hunger and leaven.[66] A requested exorcism is described as "throwing the children's *bread* to the dogs" (Mark 7:27). Jesus' passion is *"drinking the cup"* (Mark 10:38). Herod's deeds are *"leaven"* (a rotting lump that corrupts everything it touches; Mark 8:15).

Significantly, the only miracle that is found in all four gospels is one involving food: the story of Jesus' feeding the five thousand (Mark 6:34–44; Matthew 14:13–21; Luke 9:10b–17; John 6:1–15). It is obvious that the evangelists (each in his own distinctive way) saw a link between the miraculous multiplication of loaves and fishes and the traditions of Christian eucharist (note the "took, blessed, broke, gave" language of the feeding stories). Lee Klosinksi has suggested that "this juxtaposition of miracle and euchar-ist" is a parabolic maneuver designed to shake hearers/ readers into new ways of thinking about both miraculous deeds and eucharistic fellowship.[67]

There are two keys to this parabolic rethinking. The first is the unusual nature of Jesus' deed—multiplying food. For although miracle stories were common stock in the ancient world, virtually none of them ever took miraculous multi-plications of food as a theme. The second key is extrava-gance —the huge crowd, the small number of loaves and fishes, yet the resulting satisfaction of the hungry ("they all ate and were satisfied!" Mark 6:42). This combination of strange theme and extravagant result stretches the bound-aries of "the real" and "the possible" to the breaking point. Moreover, from the reader's viewpoint, the story's decisive element—just how did Jesus accomplish this extraordinary feat?—is never described! Readers are required to supply their own conclusions about the manner in which the miracle was accomplished.

Further complicating matters for the reader is the presence of familiar eucharistic language in the story (Jesus "took the five loaves . . . said the blessing . . . broke them and gave them . . ." Mark 6:41). The reader naturally begins wondering what the connections are between this miraculous multiplication of food and the eucharistic meals of the community. And that is exactly the point of the story's parabolic strategy. As virtually all scholars agree, one can already discern in the New Testament itself a movement away from concern about community meals to concern with cultic moments and cultic elements (most specifically, with the elements of bread and wine identified with Jesus' body and blood and interpreted in terms of his saving death for all). But by repeating the "taking, blessing, breaking, giving" language in the miraculous feeding stories, the evangelists have redirected attention to the meaning of Jesus' other meals (and not just the Last Supper). Indeed, Mark's redirection of attention to the *eucharistic* significance of loaves and fishes is even more emphatic, because for him the Last Supper is *not* meant to be a repeated event (it is, rather, the culmination of his theme about the disciples' failure to understand and an interpretation of Jesus' death in light of the martyrological tradition as a saving event).[68]

This bringing together of diverse elements—a bizarre story, an incredibly extravagant deed done within a eucharistic atmosphere—thus creates a parabolic conflict that requires readers to relinquish their exclusive focus on the highly cultic images of the Last Supper and to redirect attention to the memory and meaning of those meals in which Jesus healed the hungry and responded immediately to real human needs through the extravagant gestures of loaves and fishes. In other words, these stories challenge Christians to remember that eucharistic origins lie *not* in Jesus' *last* meal, but in all those events wherein Jesus (as either guest or host) satisfied hunger, announced the unbridled joy of God's arrival in the present moment

("God's reign"), and provided healing and hope for the poor and needy.

A similar challenge occurs in stories like that of the anointing at Bethany (Mark 14:3–9). In this story, too, readers are confronted by an outrageous and extravagant situation. Jesus is at table in the home of a leper (unclean!), when a woman (unclean! immoral!) bearing an alabaster jar of very expensive perfume comes to him. Taking the jar, she breaks it, and pours the perfume on Jesus' feet (there's that "taking/breaking/giving" language again!). Note well: Mark's story of the Last Supper contained no command to repeat; but this story, of a woman's extravagant gesture of hospitality in the context of a meal, is to be repeated "wherever the gospel is proclaimed . . . in memory of her." The point is unmistakable. The woman's extravagant deed of service and love is the true meaning of eucharistic dining (as opposed to the greed and narrow-minded bickering of the onlookers in the story).[69]

A fifth meaning of "Do this in memory of me" is thus *"Do this in memory of her!* Make your eucharistic table a place of lavish abundance and extravagant service, where the tired, the poor, the hungry and all who, driven by despair and need, may find real food, real rest, real comfort, real nurture." Perhaps it is time for us to wonder if our essentially *cultic* eucharist has not blinded us to its broader and more basic meaning. As church historian Peter Brown has noted, one of the most far-reaching decisions in religious history was Christianity's choice to abandon a eucharist of abundance in favor of one that stressed interpersonal bonding over access to food and drink. Perhaps we should take another look at loaves and fishes. In Brown's words:

> A Christian church, patronized largely by the well-fed and increasingly led by austere men . . . whose restricted diet was the result of choice and not of necessity, found itself, in the next centuries, increasingly tempted to treat sexuality (a drive which frequently assumes leisure and regular eating habits), rather than and famine, as the most abiding and disquieting symptom of the

frailty of the human condition. Maybe the time has come to look again at the seemingly absurd dreams of abundance of ancient Mediterranean men, to find, through their concerns, one way, at least, to more humane and more commonsensical objects of anxiety.[70]

As Christian history unfolded, then, attention shifted. Jesus' focus on open commensality (a meal practice that emphasized radical egalitarianism, inclusivity and abundance) was replaced by a focus on Jesus himself. The bread-breaker became the bread broken. Concern for cultic moments and cultic elements replaced concern for feeding the five thousand, for multiplying loaves and fishes on behalf of the hungry. Gradually the *community* meal itself (as a time of joyful assembly, feasting, care of the needy, and instruction) assumed less importance, and a cultic *eucharistic* meal (with emphasis on the bread and cup as Christ's body and blood) grew ever more significant. (This eucharistic tradition was already familiar to Paul, who links the elements of broken bread and poured-out wine to Jesus' saving death.) Perhaps our challenge today is to do as Mark did, to refocus our understanding of *Last* Supper by relocating its eucharistic significance in the meals through which Jesus brought real food to the hungry, real healing to the sick, and real rest to the weary.

Chapter Three

The Eucharistic Theology of the Rite of Christian Initiation of Adults

■

Chapter two began with a meditation on the Easter Vigil as a ritual re-creation of the world. The sacraments of Christian initiation, celebrated in the holy night of Pascha, signal our entrance into that re-created world. And that world's geography has became clearer, I hope, with our exploration of Jesus' table ministry, of his eucharistic teaching and praxis, of his revolutionary emphasis on "open commensality," egalitarianism, inclusivity and abundance.

Along the way, too, we saw that the anthropology of food is central to an understanding of who we are—as humans, as Christians. As Lee Edward Klosinski puts it,

> Food has the capacity both to serve as the object of human transactions and to symbolize human interaction, relationships and relatedness. Giving and receiving food creates obligations. It involves the creation of matrices of reciprocity and mutuality. It defines relationships and the contours of group boundaries.[1]

We are—quite literally—what, how, how much, and with whom we eat! Table is the place where a community's quintessential identity is revealed and reaffirmed. Not surprisingly, then, the acts by which a Christian is made (not born!) conclude at the communal table, in acts of eating and drinking.

In this chapter I want to turn attention toward the eucharistic theology embedded in—or implied by—the *Rite of Christian Initiation of Adults* and to ask what is distinctive about eucharist as a sacrament of *initiation*.

The Eucharistic Norm

It is astonishing how often theology—like many other human endeavors—either starts in the wrong place, mistakes the periphery for the center, or paints itself into a corner by forgetting W. H. Auden's wise admonition that "logic is the art of going wrong, with confidence." Nowhere, perhaps, is this truer than in the case of eucharistic theology. To mention "eucharist" and "theology" in the same breath is to trip a trigger that releases a barrage of thoughts about "matter" and "form," "substance" and "accident," the relation between "signifiers" and "signified," "real symbols" *versus* "empty signs," sacrifice and sacrament, etc. This is the case because much Western sacramental thought has been a minimalist theology narrowly focused on cultic *moments* and cultic *elements*—and on what is minimally required for a valid and licit celebration. We Westerners tend to ask, "What is the exact moment of consecration?" rather than, "What is the nature of the assembly's eucharistic action and prayer?" We ask, "What happens to the bread and wine?" rather than, "What happens to the celebrating people?" We ask, "Who is authorized to preside at eucharist?" rather than, "How are God's people empowered to *become* what they celebrate—the Body of Christ, member for member?"

A related mistake comes from our habit of confusing statistical frequency with superior status (the more often it happens, the more important it must be!). In preconciliar days, for instance, the silent, "scorched-earth" low Mass was often perceived as the norm of Catholic worship simply because it was, in many places, the form of celebration most frequently experienced by churchgoers. (This, in spite of the fact that the official books clearly regarded Sunday "high Mass"—*sung* Mass celebrated by the pastor for the people—as liturgically normative.) But in fact norms are neither statistics nor public opinion polls. "A norm," as Aidan Kavanagh points out, "has nothing to do with the number of times a thing is done, but it has everything to do with the *standard* according to which a thing is done."[2] Norms are not simply ideals "all wish for but are under no obligation to realize."[3] They are principles perceived as so vital to a community's identity, stability and survival that they become the agreed-upon standard for judging behaviors, beliefs and meanings. Norms thus become the basis upon which a community transacts its business with the world, rewards fidelity or sanctions deviance and establishes boundaries.

In its pastoral documents and reformed rites, the Second Vatican Council clearly defined two norms it considered essential for life together in the church. One of these norms is ecclesiological, the other eucharistic—and each implies the other. The ecclesiological norm was enunciated in the 1963 *Constitution on the Sacred Liturgy,* paragraph 41:

> The principal manifestation (Latin: *praecipua manifestatio)* of the church consists in the full, active participation of all God's holy people in the same liturgical celebrations, especially in the same eucharist, in one prayer, at one altar, at which the bishop presides, surrounded by his college of priests and by his ministers.[4]

The eucharistic norm was stated most vigorously in the 1970 *General Instruction on the Roman Missal,* chapter 1, paragraph 1:

> The celebration of the Mass, as an action of Christ and the people of God hierarchically ordered, is the center of the whole Christian life for the universal church, the local church and for

each and every one of the faithful. For therein is the culminating action whereby God sanctified the world in Christ and Christians worship the Father . . . through Christ the Son. The mysteries of our redemption are in some way made present throughout the course of the year by the celebration of Mass. All other sacred celebrations and the activities of the Christian life are related to the Mass; they spring forth from it and culminate in it.[5]

The theological implication of these two intimately connected norms was recognized even before the Council by theologian Karl Rahner. The eucharist is not simply something the church does from time to time—one act among many others; rather, it *constitutes* the church, creates it, actualizes it, brings it into being.

In the eucharist God's gracious, unrepentant, salvific will for all men [and women] becomes present, tangible and visible in this world, because it turns the tangible, visible community of the faithful (the church) into that sign which does not simply point to a grace and salvific will of God that may exist somewhere, but *is* the tangibility and permanence of this grace and of salvation. Thus the sacrament of the eucharist and the sacramentality of the church are intimately connected.[6]

In the eucharist, the church becomes what it celebrates: the visible, tangible, permanent presence of God's saving grace poured out in and for the world through the death and resurrection of Jesus. That is why the eucharist is, at one and the same time, "the sacrament of the most radical and real presence of the Lord and the fullest actualization of the essence of the church."[7]

No church without eucharist; no eucharist without church. The ecclesiological and eucharistic norms enunciated by the Second Vatican Council are thus inseparable. Just as the *church* is constituted by the full, active participation of all God's people in the same eucharist, in one prayer, at one altar, so the *eucharist* is never to be regarded as anything less than an act of the *whole* church, head and members:

The eucharist is never a matter of a bishop's or presbyter's own feelings or piety alone: It is never "his Mass." Nor is the sacrifice of the New Covenant ever merely a matter of contractual obligation between private parties in the church. Rather, it is always the church being most itself in public, obedient to the Lord's command to "do this for my remembrance," in a manner worthy of his Body at once ecclesial and sacramental.[8]

In a nutshell, if the norm (i.e., the standard against which everything else is judged) of church is eucharist, the norm of eucharist is the feasting that completes the paschal sacraments. If eucharist is the place we must go if we want to see "the church being most itself in public," then the Easter Vigil's feast is the place we must go if we want to see "the eucharist being most itself in public." For the eucharist is most truly itself when the assembly gathers during that "night when heaven is wedded to earth" to re-create the world in fire and word, water and food. On that night, the eucharist is seen most fully for what it is: the Easter sacrament, the memorial of the cross, the presence of the Risen One, the completion of Christian initiation, the foretaste of the eternal Pasch, the consummate act of priesthood exercised by God's holy people. All this is beautifully summarized in the 1988 circular letter of the Congregation for Divine Worship on "Preparing and Celebrating the Paschal Feasts":

> The celebration of the eucharist forms the fourth part of the (paschal) vigil and marks its high point, for it is in the fullest sense the Easter sacrament, that is to say, the commemoration of the sacrifice of the cross and the presence of the risen Christ, the completion of Christian initiation and the foretaste of the eternal Pasch.
>
> Great care should be taken that this eucharistic liturgy is not celebrated in haste; indeed, all the rites and words must be given their full force: the general intercessions, in which for the first time the neophytes now as members of the faithful exercise their priesthood; the procession at the offertory, in which the neophytes . . . take part; the first, second or third eucharistic prayer, preferably sung, with their proper embolisms; and finally eucharistic communion, as the moment of full participation in the mystery that is being celebrated.[9]

The Easter Vigil's table is not "just another eucharist"; it is the standard that defines the meaning of everything else—cross and sacrifice, memorial and presence, ministry and priesthood, intercession and prayer, participation and communion.

We can understand, therefore, why the eucharist is always the culminating act in the sacramental sequence of Christian initiation. Having been plunged into the waters and sealed with the Spirit's gifts, neophytes are led to the table where the community of believers *becomes* the visible presence of God's grace, becomes food and drink *for the world's life.* For the church is not simply "grace made visible" for its own sake; it is, as the Council insisted, the *sacramentum mundi*—the visible, effective embodiment of the whole world's destiny to become "people of God." Church is sacrament—and because it is sacrament, it is mission. This point is explicitly noticed—and explicitly linked to the initiatory eucharist—in the *General Introduction* to Christian Initiation:

> Finally, coming to the table of the eucharist, we eat the flesh and drink the blood of the Son of Man so that we may have eternal life and show forth the unity of God's people. By offering ourselves with Christ we share in the universal sacrifice, that is, the entire community of the redeemed offer to God by their High Priest, and *we pray for a greater outpouring of the Holy Spirit, so that the whole human race may be brought into the unity of God's family.*[10]

Eucharist completes the sacraments of initiation precisely because it establishes the church's identity and mission as sacrament of God's presence and sacrament of the world's destiny. "Thus the three sacraments of Christian initiation," says the *General Introduction,* "closely combine . . . *to enable us to carry out the mission of the entire people of God in the church and in the world.*" For in God's plan it is not just believers but all creation, redeemed and transfigured, that is destined to feast at table in the presence of God. Christians are called not to be the czars of a new creation, but its servants—the kitchen help, the table waiters. It is our job to gather up whatever needs gathering, to feed whatever needs feeding, to hold whatever needs holding, to love whatever needs loving, to heal whatever needs healing—so that all may experience the world as a wedding. It is our job to let creation take possession of us so that, in all our earthly walk, the left foot cries "Glory!" as the right foot cries "Amen!" The eucharistic elements are not only eschatological (i.e., pointing to the final destiny of our species and planet), they are cosmic (i.e., pertaining to the life and destiny of all the universe). By eating the tiny elements of eucharist, we eat the whole world—welcoming its life into our bodies, just as Christ has welcomed ours into his. There is a wonderful passage in Annie Dillard's book *Pilgrim at Tinker Creek* that captures this insight:

> I think that the dying pray at the last not "please," but *"thank you,"* as a guest thanks his host at the door. . . . The universe was not made in jest but in solemn incomprehensible earnest. By a power that is unfathomably secret, and holy, and fleet. There is nothing to be done about it, but ignore it, or see. And then you walk fearlessly, eating what you must, growing wherever you can, like the monk on the road who knows precisely how vulnerable he is, who takes no comfort among death-forgetting men, and who carries his vision of vastness and might around in his tunic like a live coal. . . .
>
> Power broods, spins, and lurches down. The planet and the power meet with a shock. They fuse and tumble, lightning, ground fire; they part, mute, submitting, and touch again with hiss and fire. . . .
>
> Emerson saw it. "I dreamed that I floated at will in the great Ether, and I saw this world floating also not far off, but diminished to the size of an apple. Then an angel took it in his hand and brought it to me and said, 'This must thou eat.' And I ate the world." All of it. All of it intricate, speckled, gnawed, fringed, and free. Israel's priests offered the wave breast and the heave shoulder together, freely, in full knowledge, for thanksgiving. They waved, they heaved, and neither gesture was whole without the other and both meant a wide-eyed and keen-eyed *thanks.*[11]

111

Eating the eucharist is eating the world. The newly initiated Christian is not being welcomed into a separatist cult that sees itself as a community of the pure, appointed by God to judge and condemn the world. Rather, the neophytes are led from the murky and unfamiliar mysteries of the water into a room ablaze with light, where the gathered assembly offers them the culturally familiar and humanly comforting signs of table and meal. If death in the baptismal waters took the neophytes out of this world, eating in the eucharistic hall returns them to it—to its labor, its abundant produce, its ripeness, its weariness and need, its plenty. (Is this the reason why, in an earlier age, Christians heaped their eucharistic tables not only with bread and wine, but also with milk and honey, olives, cheese and oil, vegetables and fruits for feeding the poor?) Neophytes have not been asked to reject the world—but to reject *sin,* the glamour of *evil, Satan's* works and empty promises.

Mystery thus leads inevitably to mission. Eucharist leads not to the world's rejection but to the world's *recovery.* It is not merely idle theological rhetoric, then, to say that "the three sacraments of Christian initiation closely combine . . . to enable us to carry out the mission of the entire people of God in the Church and in the world." That is why the Christian mission was conceived by the Second Vatican Council (in its "Decree on the Apostolate of Lay People") not merely as a religious enterprise but as a worldly one as well:

> The mission of the church . . . is not only to bring men and women the message and grace of Christ but also to permeate and improve the whole range of the temporal. The laity, carrying out this mission . . . exercise their apostolate therefore in the world as well as in the church, in the temporal order as well as in the spiritual. These orders are distinct; they are nevertheless so closely linked that *God's plan is, in Christ, to take the whole world up again and make of it a new creation.*[12]

This mission of renewing the world, of recovering creation for God, is rooted in baptismal regeneration and sustained by the community's regular recourse to eucharist. The Council's "Decree on the Church's Missionary Activity" makes this point forcefully:

> The Holy Spirit calls all to Christ through the seed of the word and the preaching of the gospel and inspires in hearts the obedience of faith. . . . In the womb of the baptismal font the Spirit gives birth into a new life to those who believe . . . gathering them all together into the one people of God. . . .
>
> As God's co-workers, missionaries are to create congregations of believers of a kind that . . . will carry out the divinely appointed offices of priest, prophet and ruler. This is how the Christian community becomes a sign of God's presence in the world: by the eucharistic sacrifice it goes constantly with Christ to God; strengthened by the Word, it bears witness to Christ; it walks in charity and burns with the apostolic spirit. Right from the beginning the Christian community should be trained to be as far as possible self-sufficient in regard to its own needs.[13]

The twin norms of ecclesiology and eucharist thus give rise to the twin activities of mission and ministry. As there is no church without eucharist, so there is no eucharist without mission. To eat and drink the Supper is to eat and drink the world; to let the Lord in is to let the world in—a point developed beautifully by Kathleen Raine in her "Northumbrian Sequence IV":

Let in the wind
Let in the rain
Let in the moors tonight,

The storm beats on my window-pane
Night stands at my bed-foot
Let in the fear,
Let in the pain,
Let in the trees and toss and groan . . .

Fearful is my virgin heart
And frail my virgin form,
And must I then take pity on
The raging of the storm
That rose up from the great abyss
Before the earth was made,
That pours the stars in cataracts
And shakes this violent world?

Let in the fire,
Let in the power,
Let in the invading might . . .

Let in the wound,
Let in the pain,
Let in your child tonight.[14]

The Liturgy of the World

The purpose of the eucharist, then, is not to create a community closed off from the world, but to sustain one that embraces, fully and boldly, what Karl Rahner liked to call "the liturgy of the world." For as Rahner understood it, the world's history is itself a liturgy—indeed, it is the *original liturgy*. In a memorable passage of extraordinary power and beauty, Rahner explains just what constitutes this original liturgy of the world:

> The world and its history are the terrible and sublime liturgy, breathing of death and sacrifice, which God celebrates and causes to be celebrated in and through human history in its freedom. . . . In the entire length and breadth of this immense history of birth and death, complete superficiality, folly, inadequacy and hatred (all of which "crucify") on the one hand, and silent submission, responsibility . . . attaining the heights and plumbing the depths, on the other, the true liturgy of the world is present—present in such a way that the liturgy which [Christ] has brought to its absolute fullness on his cross belongs intrinsically to it.[15]

It is this whole tumultuous history of human experience—charged with human grandeur and folly, gripped by grace at its roots, crowned by the cross of Christ—that creates the liturgy of the world.

Two Views of Grace   Rahner's understanding of the liturgy of the world (and its relation to the church's public worship) is based on the contrast between two very different views of grace—of the way God's life and human history intersect. One view, which dominated Roman

Catholic thought on the subject prior to Vatican II, sees the world, at best, as neutral and secular or, at worst, as sinful, godless and graceless. According to this view, God's grace appears as an *intervention* in the world's history, as something that disrupts the ordinary flow of sinful, secular life. Sacraments are seen "as events . . . where grace comes to be in a world otherwise deprived of it."[16]

But there is another way of looking at the relation between the world and grace. It starts with the assumption that "the secular world from the outset is always encompassed and permeated with the grace of [God's] self-communication. This grace is always and everywhere present in the world."[17]

This second view assumes that ever since the Big Bang (and before), there never has been a moment when "pure nature" existed. On the contrary, from the first nano-seconds of its existence, the universe has been saturated with God's grace and presence. From that very first moment of roaring fire and light, splitting atoms and thermal fusion, God has been seeking, in love, to impart the divine self. Far from being a neutral cipher, nature is precisely that reality upon which God's life can be bestowed in free love. In Rahner's felicitous phrase, "Nature is, because grace has to be. . . . Nature is never purely and simply secular; it is always nature graciously endowed with God's self."[18]

The history of the world, then, "must be understood . . . in a true and radical sense as the history of God."[19] Given this view of grace, the sacraments are not interventions — occasional forays of a gunslinging God in a wicked world — but *outbursts,* shouts and exclamations that point to the ever-present grace of God already and always taking possession of the whole world's history, its length and breadth. This means, of course, that grace occurs not only (or primarily) in the sacraments, but wherever a person freely accepts and embraces existence as a radical gift utterly dependent on God. In other words, grace occurs, as poet Pablo Neruda once wrote, wherever we accept and embrace the confused impurity of the human condition . . . footprints and fingerprints, the abiding presence of the human engulfing all artifacts. . . .

A poetry impure as the clothing we wear, or our bodies, soup-stained, soiled with our shameful behavior, our wrinkles and vigils and dreams . . . the shocks of encounter, political loyalties, denials and doubts, affirmations and taxes.

The holy canons of madrigal, the mandates of touch, smell, taste, sight, hearing, the passion for justice, sexual desire, the sea sounding . . . the deep penetration of things in the transports of love.[20]

The church's worship does not try to compete with, intrude upon, or sacralize the liturgy of the world. Rather, through embodied symbols, the church seeks to make what is always going on in the liturgy of the world tangible, explicit and conscious. It is not, after all, obvious to most of us that the world is possessed and permeated by grace; on the contrary, we often feel bludgeoned by its relentless banality, its harsh cruelty and indifference to suffering, its schemes and stupidity. Nor is it obvious that the long history of the world's freedom reaches an irreversible climax in the cross of Christ (which has determined that our species' destiny is a destiny of salvation and grace, not of destruction and death). We need, then, some embodied, ritual and symbolic means of rendering that history of grace palpable and real.

And that is what the church's worship does: It *renders visible, names, claims and celebrates* the divine depth that sustains ordinary life—even when that life seems wearisome, vapid, meaningless, cheap, loveless and altogether too painful to bear. The church's worship does not claim to give people an experience that never occurs anywhere else (a mistake to which the "talk-show" model of liturgy is particularly prone). Rather, it seeks to identify and appropriate the wondrous mystery and grace that surround us always, even when we are not aware of them.

When we say that we celebrate the death of the Lord until he returns, we are saying that we are giving space and time explicitly in our own life to the culmination of the history of the world liturgy which is present in the cross of Jesus. . . . Consequently what happens in worship of this kind is . . . something that occurs always and everywhere . . . for all time and . . . everywhere in the world, and is explicitly celebrated, stated and appropriated. This ecclesial worship is important . . . not because something happens in it that does not happen elsewhere, but because there is present . . . in it that which makes the world important, since it is everywhere blessed by grace, by faith, hope and love, and in it there occurred the cross of Christ, which is the culmination of its engraced history.[21]

The mysticism of everyday life   To put it another way, we will never experience the church's liturgy as a life-giving encounter with Mystery until we first touch "the experience of God hidden in the midst of our daily lives."[22] It is for this reason that Rahner spoke, in his later works, of the need for "a mystagogy of the mysticism of ordinary life."[23] It was his conviction that every human experience—no matter how mundane, ordinary and limiting it seems—has the potential to bring us to the threshold of Mystery. In order for these experiences to put us in touch with God, they do not have to be analyzed or articulated in overtly religious terms. In fact, most people today experience God in ways that are not explicitly religious (if by "religion" one means the rarefied world of worship, prayer and theological speculation). As Pablo Neruda suggested, God is experienced, instead, in "the confused impurity of the human condition—in the weight of mineral; the light of honey; the sound of the words 'night' and 'goodbye'; the shades of wheat, ivory and tears; objects of leather, wool or wood; faded, aged things that gather around our lives like walls."[24] God is experienced when "I" notice that

there is this sound:
a red noise of bones,
a clashing of flesh,
and yellow legs like merging spikes of grain.
I listen among the smack of kisses,
I listen, shaken between gasps and sobs.

I am looking, hearing,
with half my soul upon the sea and half my soul upon the land,
and with the two halves of my soul I look at the world.

And though I close my eyes and cover my heart entirely,
I see a muffled waterfall,
in big muffled raindrops,
It is like a hurricane of gelatine,
like a waterfall of sperm and jellyfish.
I see a turbid rainbow form.
I see its waters pass across the bones.[25]

The smack of kisses . . . gasps and sobs . . . half the soul on the sea, half on the land . . . water passing across bone: These are the ways most of us experience God. They are not ways that announce themselves as "spiritual" or "religious," yet they are. That is the point of Rahner's "mysticism of ordinary life." They are moments of wonder, beauty, goodness, grace and peace; moments of doubt and fear; moments of limitation, loathing, loneliness, pain and isolation; moments of resentment and anger. They occur whenever we remain faithful to a commitment, despite what it costs us; whenever we forgive someone who has broken our heart; whenever we love and accept a child for who she is, rather than for what we wanted her to be; whenever we ladle lentils in a soup kitchen instead of complaining about the high cost of welfare programs; whenever we confront death advancing in the body of one we love; whenever our confusion, pain and anger force us, finally, to make a change.

Many of these are experiences of limitation. But as Michael Skelley points out,

> Precisely because these are such powerful experiences of limita-
> tion, they can be equally powerful experiences of transcen-
> dence. We could not experience these limits as limits unless we
> were also able to go beyond them. . . . To know that we have
> limits but to perceive that there is something beyond those
> limits is to experience transcendence. To perceive that there is
> something beyond our limits and to affirm the good we may
> glimpse only dimly there is to experience God. And to do this

again and again is to gradually discover that God is present in every experience, no matter how negative.[26]

To sum it up, just as "grace presupposes nature," the liturgy of the church presupposes the liturgy of the world. Worship cannot lead us into the precincts of Mystery unless the "mystagogy of the mysticism of ordinary life" has led us to recognize God's abiding presence in our "irreligious" lives and in our "secular" world. While the church's rites remain important and necessary symbolic embodiments of God's presence in *all* our moments, they are not intended to be grandiose "Super Bowls" of grace. On the contrary, sacraments — the eucharist, especially — are small signs, humble landmarks erected to proclaim that the *entire world* belongs to God; that the presence of grace (God's self-bestowal) is limitless; that the world is constantly and ceaselessly possessed by God from its innermost roots, from the personal center of every human being; that God's self-giving does not depend on our ability or willingness to name this experience "religious" and that one "spiritual."[27]

Indeed, this is the whole point of that "mystagogy" which the *Rite of Christian Initiation of Adults* assumes will follow once the sacraments of initiation have been brought to completion in eucharist:

> This is a time for the community and the neophytes together to grow in deepening their grasp of the paschal mystery and in making it part of their lives through meditation on the gospel, sharing in the eucharist and doing the works of charity.[28]

The kind of knowing that *mystagogia* imparts is not derived, of course, from theological syllabi but from the sharpened recognition that all human experience is ripe with potential for experiencing God. Perhaps the Christian neophyte, fed by eucharist and enlightened by mystagogy, can address to God the words Pablo Neruda once addressed to his long-time friend Alberto Rojas Jiménez:

> Beneath the tombs, beneath the ashes,
> beneath the frozen snails,

119

beneath the last terrestrial waters,
you come flying.

Farther down, among . . .
blind plants, and broken fish,
farther down, among clouds again,
you come flying.

Beyond blood and bones,
beyond bread, beyond wine,
beyond fire,
you come flying.

Beyond vinegar and death,
among putrefaction and violets,
with your celestial voice and your damp shoes,
you come flying.[29]

Recovering Vision

The community of those who gather to *do* eucharist
(for eucharist is indeed a verb long before it is a noun) is,
then, a community formed by "the mystagogy of the
mysticism of everyday life." It is a community whose eyes
have been opened to see God "come flying . . . beyond
vinegar and death, among putrefaction and violets." Indeed,
recovering vision is central to the ongoing conversion
process which eucharist is designed to nurture and sustain.
As the seventeenth-century poet and mystic Thomas Traherne wrote in his *Centuries:*

> Insatiableness is good, but not ingratitude . . .
> You will never enjoy the world aright, till you see how a sand
> exhibiteth the wisdom and power of God . . .
> Your enjoyment of the world is never right till every
> morning you awake in heaven . . . and look upon the skies and
> the earth and the air as celestial joys . . .
> You will never enjoy the world aright till the sea itself
> floweth in your veins, till you are clothed with the heavens, and
> crowned with the stars, and perceive yourself to be the sole heir
> of the whole world . . .
> Till your spirit filleth the whole world, and the stars are your
> jewels, till you are as familiar with the ways of God in all ages as
> with your walk and table.[30]

Doing eucharist is meant to lead the baptized toward a recovery of precisely this sort of vision. For as I indicated earlier in this chapter, eating the eucharist means eating the world—surrendering to it as the privileged place where God's grace is known, where Christ's cross is raised as history's climax, and where the Spirit is poured out upon *all* flesh (i.e., upon the entire human enterprise, understood in its condition of weakness and need). It is difficult to surrender to the world, however, if we don't know what's there, if our eye has never taken a keen inventory of its contents, if our blood and bones have never entered "the harsh cathedral of gentle matter." The eucharist, after all, is a *sacrifice*—the embodied symbol of Jesus' surrender not only to death but to everything that lends death its meaning and its terror. It is easy to imagine these words on the lips of Jesus as he hung dying, surrendering to the whole historical process by which the world's life is handed over to the Mystery of God:

> I am the one facing your wave of dying fragrances,
> wrapped in autumn and resistance:
> I am the one undertaking a funereal voyage
> among your yellow scars:
> I am the one with my sourceless laments,
> foodless, abandoned, alone,
> entering darkened corridors,
> reaching your mysterious substance. . . .
>
> Come to me, to my measureless dream,
> fall into my bedroom where night falls
> and endlessly falls like broken water,
> and bind me to your life and to your death . . .
> let us make fire, and silence, and sound,
> and let us burn, and be silent, and bells.[31]

In the eucharistic sacrifice Christians embrace Jesus' death—and by so doing, they embrace the whole history of his obedient surrender to that "One who could save him from death" (Hebrews 5:7). The eucharist is thus a school of surrender, where we learn to look the world full in the face—with all its dying fragrances, measureless dreams and broken water—and to bind ourselves fearlessly to its mysteries of life and death. As Jesus did. For by surrendering to the cross, Jesus not only gave himself up to the malevolent powers of repression and violence; he also embraced all the natural processes of historical evolution. It was this latter point that intrigued the great twentieth-century Jesuit paleontologist Pierre Teilhard de Chardin:

> I believe that the universe is an evolution. I believe that evolution proceeds toward spirit. I believe that in man [and woman], spirit is fully realized in person. I believe that the supremely personal is . . . Christ.[32]

In a word, the evolving dynamism of history and nature is fully revealed only when matter becomes living and conscious, reflective and free—only when matter can finally see God through the eyes of Christ.[33] "This is my body" does not simply mean "this bread has become what I am"; it means that Jesus has identified himself wholly with the full range of history's potential and its limits (of which bread is the humble sign). As Chardin expressed it:

> Since first, Lord, you said "This is my body," not only the bread of the altar but (to some degree) everything in the universe that nourishes the soul for the life of Spirit and Grace has become yours and has become divine—it is divinized, divinizing and divinizable. Every presence makes me feel that you are near me; every touch is the touch of your hand; every necessity transmits to me a pulsation of your will. And so true is this, that everything around me that is essential and enduring has become for me . . . the substance of your heart: Jesus![34]

By embracing death, Jesus was "eating the world," surrendering fully and irrevocably to its history—and thus becoming forever linked to its destiny. For death is not simply life's (involuntary) end, it is the beginning of matter's transformation. In a passage that echoes Chardin, Karl Rahner once wrote,

> We Christians are . . . the most sublime of materialists. We recognize and believe that this matter will last for ever, and be glorified for ever. It must be glorified. It must undergo a

transformation the depths of which we can only sense with fear and trembling in that process which we experience as our death. But it remains. It continues to perform its function for ever. It celebrates a festival that lasts for ever.[35]

The fermentation that will transfigure the world has already begun in the death and rising of Jesus. For through the paschal mystery the divine dynamism that causes this transformation has already been released upon the world. This dynamism has a name; it is, as Paul says, the Spirit of God, the "first installment" of creation's destiny (see 2 Corinthians 5:1–5; Romans 8:18–27); the same Spirit who hovered over the primordial chaos; who will preserve and transform all things that were and are; whose power is invoked upon elements and people in the eucharist to make them "one body, one spirit in Christ." It is this power that has now become present at the center of all things:

> This power of all powers, this meaning which is the ultimate meaning of all meanings, is now present at the very heart and centre of all reality including material reality, and has already, in the glorified flesh of the Son, brought the beginning of the world triumphantly to its final goal of perfection. . . . The festival we are celebrating is an eschatological one. In this celebration we anticipate . . . the universal and glorious trans-figuration of the world which has already commenced, and which, since the ascension, has been ripening and developing towards the point where it will become manifest.[36]

Recovering our vision means reclaiming the ability to see the world as precisely that place which is ripening toward a final destiny in the presence of God. That is why the eucharist consecrates *things,* not ideas. The transforma-tion of bread and wine becomes the embodied symbol of that still greater transfiguration that awaits the whole creation. So, in traditional Catholic theology, it is one and the same Spirit who works to accomplish a fourfold transformation: *personal* (the raising of Jesus "in the Spirit": 1 Peter 3:18); *sacramental* (the Spirit invoked to transform the gifts of bread and wine); *collective* (the Spirit invoked to transform the assembly); and *cosmic* (the Spirit will transfigure all of "groaning creation": Romans 8:22–23). It is precisely because of the Spirit's presence and action that the death of Jesus is not simply a violent murder but a living sacrifice that redeems the world (i.e., opens the world fully to God's transfiguring presence and so restores its potential to become a "new creation": 2 Corinthians 5:17).

How does the Christian participate in this "living sacrifice"? By surrendering. By letting go of the compulsion to control the world's creatures and to manipulate history's outcome. That is why the great sacrificial act of the Christian assembly is neither ritual slaughter nor strategic planning but *eucharistia,* a sacrifice of thanksgiving that returns all of created reality to its source in the Spirit. For in the face of God's extravagant gestures of creation and salvation, all the Christian can do is praise, acknowledge, surrender, serve, bear witness and open the self like a shutter to receive the light. Only then is the Christian afforded an intuition of what a world in transformation looks and feels, sounds and tastes like. Annie Dillard has described how this letting go transfigures our sense of seeing. "There is another kind of seeing," she writes, "that involves a letting go. When I see this way I sway transfixed and emptied." To make her point clearer, she describes what happened to her one evening near sundown as she watched pale petals floating on a creek's surface:

> I blurred my eyes and gazed towards the brim of my hat and saw a new world. I saw the pale white circles roll up, roll up, like the world's turning, mute and perfect, and I saw the linear flashes, gleaming silver, like stars being born at random down a rolling scroll of time. Something broke and something opened. I filled up like a new wineskin. I breathed an air like light; I saw a light like water. I was the lip of a fountain the creek filled forever; I was ether, the leaf in the zephyr; I was flesh-flake, feather, bone.
>
> When I see this way I see truly. As Thoreau says, I return to my senses.[37]

Surrender is the only way we can "return to our senses," the only way our selves can be broken open and filled with the first fruits of a new creation. And so, in the assembly's eucharistic prayer, every created being and every historical event—from the highest order of angel to the simplest coelenterate; from creation's dawn to Christ's cross and beyond—is returned to its Source as praise and thanksgiving. In the eucharistic action, the assembly at last returns to its senses: its eyes illumined by letting go; its ears opened to human utterance as God's Word; its belly buoyed by bread and wine become flesh and blood; its tongue loosened by the breath of Silence; its touch restored by the ancient gestures of folding, holding, lifting, joining. All this comes to an ecstatic climax in the crashing chorus that concludes the opening portion of the eucharistic prayer: "Holy! Holy! Holy!"

> Holy is your name!
> Holy is your work!
> Holy are the days that return to you!
> Holy are the years that you uncover!
> Holy are the hands that are raised to you,
>   and the weeping that is wept to you!
> Holy is the fire between your will and ours,
>   in which we are refined!
> Holy is that which is unredeemed, covered with your patience!
> Holy are the souls lost in your unnaming!
> Holy, and shining with a great light, is every living thing,
>   established in this world and covered with time,
>   until your name is praised forever![38]

Welcoming the Stranger

If the eucharistic table is the place where the assembly returns to its senses, recovers its vision and recognizes the world's transfiguration as already begun in the broken vessel of Jesus' body, raised aloft in the Spirit, so that table is also the place where strangers are welcome. At first this may sound like an odd thing to say. After all, isn't the ultimate purpose of Christian initiation to form community? And isn't community a place of personal warmth and friendship, where names are known, estrangement is overcome and individuals cherished? Isn't the parish a family, fed by a common vision, committed to common goals, animated by common values?

Perhaps not. In his book *The Company of Strangers,* Parker Palmer draws two important parallels. The first concerns the parallel between religion and public life.[39]

The second concerns the manner in which our images of religious community ("church") are formed in reaction to what we feel is happening (or failing to happen) in the larger society.[40] Both these parallels have an effect on our understanding (and expectations) of community as formed by eucharist.

Religion and Public Life   At bottom, as Palmer notes, both of them have to do with *unity,* with overcoming divisiveness and fragmentation, with creating a climate in which what is broken can be healed and what is estranged can be reconciled.[41] Both the secular notion of a "common weal" and the Christian vision of "God's reign" presuppose a movement toward convergence, just as both presuppose that we are called into relationship not only with friends and family but with a larger community of persons as well. As the Germans like to say, *alles Sein ist Mit-Mensch-Sein*— all being is being-with-others. And this public life, which is essential to a definition of the human, is characterized precisely by the coming together of strangers—on elevators and subways, on streets and sidewalks, in malls and supermarkets, in lines at the bank and at the post office. Public life is a constant meeting of strangers—hence the need for those micro- and macro-rituals of decorum and civility that govern face-to-face behavior, even (or especially) when it is anonymous. (For one of civic ritual's primary purposes is to render difficult or impersonal business less risky.) As Palmer observes, public life is even more primary than politics:

It existed long before political institutions were developed and refined; and a healthy political process (at least, the process we call democracy) depends on the preexistence of a healthy public life. As important as it is to attempt to influence the government, it is even more important to renew the life of the public. Without a public which knows that it shares a common life, which is capable of feeling, thinking, debating, and deciding, politics becomes a theatre of illusion. . . . Public life creates the community which both establishes legitimate government and holds it accountable to what the people want.[42]

What all of this means, of course, is that the survival and success of public life depends on our willingness and ability to transact vital business, on a variety of levels, with strangers. And there, for many Christians, is where the parallel between public life and church community ends. For a great deal of modern ecclesiology, in practice if not in theory, relies on what Richard Sennett once called the "ideology of intimacy," a position that insists, first, that only human relationships of closeness and warmth, depth and duration have any real value; second, that nurturing such relationships requires personal skill, effort and determination; and third, that such relationships are essential for successful personality development.[43] According to this ideology, "social relationships of all kinds are believable and authentic the closer they approach the inner psychological concerns of each person . . . warmth is our god." (One can perhaps see this ideology at work in Christian liturgical celebrations where the presider desperately wants to be liked by "his public," and tries to create an atmosphere of closeness and warmth with each person in the congregation.)

For Christians, however, neither the ideology of intimacy nor the self-interest that shapes most aspects of public life is the real source of human unity. Rather, that source is to be sought in our very creation and condition as children of the same creator God. "For the Christian," writes Parker Palmer, "our unity is known not in politics but prayer, and is given by the grace which answers prayer. The unity sought by the church is not achieved through calculation and manipulation, but received through contemplation and vulnerability and self-giving."[44]

Religious Community and the Larger Society

And that leads to the second parallel: the manner in which our images of Christian community are formed by reactions to what we perceive in the larger society. This is certainly one of the reasons why the ideology of intimacy has gained such a hold on the Christian imagination. In a culture that seems overwhelmingly bureaucratic, impersonal and cold (to say nothing of dangerous, drug-ridden and violent), it is easy to see why both "authentic personhood" and "authentic community" should be seen as places of refuge, as zones of safety and warmth in a cruel and merciless world. Despite the religious right's rhetoric about "values," traditional institutions such as marriage and family are floundering; urban neighborhoods continue to decay; many schools, even in the suburbs, have become drug markets; and for many in the middle class the "American dream" has become a nightmare. In reaction to such widespread social and personal disorder, Christian communities increasingly think of themselves as oases. It is widely felt that "instead of conflict, the church should offer comfort; instead of distance between persons, intimacy; instead of criticism, affirmation and good will."[45]

In short, the church is imagined by many to be a "family." (Note how often, today, one encounters this rhetoric: "Welcome to our parish family!" "Our parish family wants to show it cares." "As members of our parish family we ask you to support . . . ") But there are serious limits to the usefulness of such an image for church life. For one thing, families offer members protections and perks not normally available in public life; for another, they often have a hard time dealing with conflict, with innovation, or with people who are "different," who don't fit the family image. A church with no room for innovators, no creative means of resolving conflict, and no tolerance for diversity and difference among its members becomes a very stagnant and unfriendly place indeed. In sum, the family model often causes churches to minimize or deny disagreements, rather than face and work through them honestly; to reward those who maintain the status quo, rather than encourage innovative thinking; and to squeeze out persons whose social, economic, ethnic or racial differences are felt to preclude our intimacy with them. The result, Parker Palmer notes, are churches that become

> preserves for people of kindred class and status. Such a church does everything in its power to eliminate the strange and cultivate the familiar. Such a church can neither welcome the stranger nor allow the stranger in each of us to emerge. Such a church is a barrier to the public life.[46]

This vision of church as refuge or oasis or preserve for people of kindred class and status has very serious—and potentially very damaging—implications for liturgical celebration. Aidan Kavanagh has drawn attention to the tendency in many American churches to baptize the values of the suburban middle class, "values such as comfort in affluence, participation in approved groups, consumerism, and a general optimism which seems to have lost its grip on reality."[47] He goes on to list some of the signs and results of this trend; these include

> the tendency to "ministerialize" the middle-class laity; to turn the entry rite into an act of gathering and hospitality conducted by such new ministers so as to produce the approved sort of community which celebrates middle-class values of joining, meeting, and "speaking out"; to use these two endeavors as means to "create community" (beyond that which the church already is by virtue of its common baptism into Christ); to move away from the art of ceremony and symbol towards verbaliza- tion as the assembly's main medium of communication within itself. Iconography is disappearing in our new church buildings, giving way to potted plants and shopping-mall-like spaces. These tendencies obscure a sense of sacramentality and of the divine presence as something distinct from and transcending the community at worship.[48]

Neither the church nor its liturgy aim at forming an intimate, homogenous fellowship of familiars united by the same socioeconomic status and espousing identical middle-class values. On the contrary, in the earliest decades of its existence the Christian movement (as represented especially by its maverick missionary Paul) consciously chose *pluralism* over parochialism. This meant that the churches would be multicultural, multi-ethnic, multiracial— places where a stranger could share a meal with strangers (just as Jesus had done in his ministry). It meant that Christian unity would result not from ideological conformity, but from welcoming "conflict as an opportunity to learn that our wholeness lies in the One who sustains us all."[49] It meant that Christian identity would result not from the suppression of diversity or difference, but from the recognition that free people can form communities "where difference does not lead to judgment, where diversity does not breed distrust."[50]

Instead of trying to create a community of the like-minded or a refuge against the perils of modern life, we need to begin building communities that are not mere extensions of private security, but bridges that connect private to public, "leading us from the familiarities of private life into the strangeness of the public realm."[51] We need to redefine church not as "family" but as "halfway house, moving people from fear of the world around them into a role as cocreators of a world which is both God's and their own."[52]

This can best be done by reaffirming Paul's bold, pluralistic blueprint for *inclusive* churches where "there is neither Jew nor Greek, slave nor free, male nor female, for all are one in Christ Jesus." Genuine pluralism does not need—or try—to homogenize experience, tame traditions, exclude innovation or devalue diversity. It begins, instead, with the recognition that no single tradition (be it biblical, Western, American or whatnot) possesses all the resources needed to deal with the bewildering challenges of modern public life. Rich as these traditions are, notes Robert Bellah,

> if we cling obstinately to them alone we will be guilty of a narrow and . . . ultimately self-destructive parochialism. We must be able to embrace the experience of the rootedness of the American Indians, the uprootedness of the Blacks, the emptiness of the Asians, not out of some charitable benevolence but because our own traditions are simply not enough. Cultural defensiveness will be fatal. *If we are to survive on this earth, we must embrace the entire human tradition, make all of it . . . available to our imagination.*[53]

Pluralism in practice rests on the conviction that each of us is incomplete, an unfinished work of art; that knowledge of God is corporate and cumulative, requiring the richest, broadest range of human experience; that ultimately each of us is a stranger—wandering, homeless, landless, at sea. Indeed, in the mind of the great American writer Herman Melville, homelessness—landlessness—is the condition that makes us images of God:

> As in landlessness alone rests highest truth, shoreless, indefinite as God—so better is it to perish in that howling infinite, than be ingloriously dashed upon the lee, even if that were safety![54]

It is a condition, so Robert Bellah writes, that "though it contains despair, invites celebration."[55] As strangers in a strange land, without home or anchor, we must begin looking for community not in the chatty, intimate circle of family and friends but

> mutely, with gesture, motion, and dance, with liturgy and sacrament. In our moral confusion and our intellectual doubt, perhaps the ordering of gesture—of the most elemental gestures, kneeling, eating, drinking, touching—is all that we are capable of. There is a natural movement from liturgy, which is communion . . . to caring and curing, to social concern.[56]

So eucharistic community arises not from the ideology of intimacy, nor from the rejection of public life, nor from middle-class values of "joining" and "participation in approved groups," but from the company of strangers, from the recognition that we are all "outside the camp," that "we have here no lasting city," that we are all "aliens, pilgrims and sojourners" (see Hebrews 11:13; 13:13–14; 1 Peter 2:11). The eucharist that completes the sacraments of Christian initiation is neither a family meal nor a graduation dinner. It is not a point of arrival, but a point of departure, not a "settling in" but a "setting out," not a homecoming but a pilgrimage:

> The eucharist . . . makes no assertion except out of negation and it sees no wholeness except out of annihilation. It is the supreme ritual expression of brokenness and death, of homelessness and landlessness. It consecrates all the good things of the earth and it promises renewal and rebirth not only for the individual but for society and the cosmos. And yet it makes us restless on this earth: It makes us see the conditional, and provisional, and broken quality of all things human.[57]

Indeed, it is precisely as a Stranger that the Risen One is met along the way, invited to table, and then (only then!) "recognized in the breaking of bread" (Luke 24:13–35). Similarly in John's gospel, it is the Stranger on the shore who invites the disciples to go fishing and to grill their catch for breakfast (John 21:1–14). The One with whom we long to break bread is precisely that One whom we do not know. In the words of the haunting hymn chanted in the Byzantine Office of Christ's Burial on Holy Saturday:

> Give me that Stranger
> Who since his youth
> Had wandered as a stranger . . .
>
> Give me that Stranger
> Upon whom I look with wonder,
> Seeing Him a Guest of Death . . .
>
> Give me that Stranger . . .
> Who being a stranger has no place
> Whereon to lay his head.

The Presence of the Absent Lord: Easter and Eucharist

It is very clear that the reforms of Christian initiation represented by the *Rite of Christian Initiation of Adults* are intimately linked to the Easter Vigil as the heart of the church year. The *sacramenta paschalia* are precisely baptism/confirmation/eucharist as these flow from the wounded Savior's side, as they unite believers to Christ's victory over sin and death, and as they are celebrated by the assembly at the "mother of all vigils." Thus the RCIA's repeated refrain about the Vigil as the proper time for initiation:

- "The Easter Vigil should be regarded as the proper time for the sacraments of initiation."[58]

- "It is hoped that, presiding if possible at the lenten liturgy, [the bishop] will himself celebrate the rite of election and, at the Easter Vigil, the sacraments of initiation."[59]

- "The sacraments themselves are celebrated at the Easter Vigil."[60]

- "The celebration of the sacraments of Christian initiation should take place at the Easter Vigil itself."[61]

- "The entire rite of Christian initiation is normally arranged so that the sacraments will be celebrated during the Easter Vigil."[62]

- "The usual time for the celebration of the sacraments of initiation is the Easter Vigil." [63]

If the heart of the church year is the Vigil, the heart of the Vigil is initiation—and the heart of initiation is eucharist. For in the minds of early Christian theologians, eucharist is that moment when neophytes celebrate, see and receive what they have become through water and the Spirit. A classic formulation of this view occurs in a sermon Augustine preached at Easter to newly baptized North Africans in Hippo, sometime between 405 and 411 CE:

133

If, then, you wish to understand the body of Christ, listen to the Apostle as he says to the faithful "You are the body of Christ and His members" (1 Corinthians 12:27). If, therefore, you are the body of Christ and His members, *your mystery has been placed on the Lord's table, you receive your mystery.* You reply "Amen" to that which you are, and by replying you consent. . . .

But why in bread? . . . "We, though many, are one bread, one body" (1 Corinthians 10:17). Understand and rejoice. Unity! Verity! Piety! Charity! "One bread." What is this one bread? "Many . . . one body." Remember that bread is not made from one grain, but from many. When you were exorcised you were, after a fashion, milled. When you were baptized you were moistened. When you received the fire of the Holy Spirit you were baked. *Be what you see, and receive what you are.* . . .

Many grapes hang in the cluster, but the liquid of the grapes is mixed in unity. So also did Christ the Lord portray us. He willed that we belong to Him. *He consecrated the mystery of our peace and unity upon His table.*[64]

For Augustine, as for many early Christians, the meaning of Easter is focused upon the mystery of the table, and the mystery of the table is nothing less than the mystery of baptized believers, who are what they see and who receive what they are—the body of Christ, member for member. Such a theology works "backwards," from sacrament to source, from table to tomb, from process/experience to event. It is the ritual action of the celebrating assembly— embodied in the sacraments of initiation—that breaks open to believers the meaning of Jesus' Pasch. It is the corporate deeds of washing, anointing, eating and drinking that put the assembly in touch with the *mysterium paschale.* For this reason most of our early Christian Easter homilies describe not so much what happened to Jesus but *what is happening to the community.* In the words of one ancient homily, whose author is unknown:

Here is the grace conferred by these heavenly mysteries, the gift which Pascha brings, the most longed-for feast of the year.

Here are the beginnings of creatures newly formed: children born from the life-giving font of holy church, born anew with the simplicity of little ones and crying out with the evidence of a clean conscience.

Here chaste fathers and pure mothers accompany this new family, countless in number, born to new life through faith.

As they emerge from the grace-giving womb of the font, a blaze of candles burns brightly beneath the cross, the tree of faith.

Here the Easter festival brings men and women the grace of holiness from heaven. Through the repeated celebration of the sacred mysteries they receive the spiritual nourishment of the sacraments.

Fostered at the very heart of holy church, the fellowship of one community worships the one God.[65]

The meaning of Easter is thus grasped by ritual performance and participation in the sacraments. "That is why," St. Leo the Great explained,

we are to celebrate the Lord's paschal sacrifice with the unleavened bread of sincerity and truth. The leaven of our former malice is thrown out, and a new creature is filled and inebriated with the Lord himself. *For the effect of our sharing in the body and blood of Christ is to change us into what we receive.* As we have died with him, and have been buried and raised to life with him, so we bear him within us, both in body and in spirit.[66]

The eucharistic experience thus puts us in touch with the event (Easter); table leads to tomb (to the discovery of what Jesus' death means); sacrament leads to source (to Jesus' dying and rising as the origin of our own rebirth).

Easter as the Story of Conversion This way of "backing into" the meaning of mysteries by returning repeatedly to the eucharistic table also reflects the way the New Testament understanding of Easter emerged. As virtually all contemporary scholars agree, the resurrection of Jesus is itself never described by the biblical writers. We are never told what happened, or when, or how; we are merely told that it happened—and that it provoked a variety of reactions, from incredulity (Thomas) to joyful recognition (Mary Magdalene). By contrast, Jesus' death (and reactions to it) are described in some detail. We are told plainly that Jesus was betrayed by an intimate friend; that he was apprehended, tried, condemned and executed in the Roman manner (by crucifixion); that the disciples' courage failed, and they fled—only to reassemble later as preachers and "witnesses."

"Easter" is thus a comprehensive name for an ensemble of events and experiences that arose between 1) Jesus' death and the disciples' flight and 2) the regathering of the disciples (often placed, by the New Testament, in the context of a *meal*). Easter, then, is not so much one event as a series of experiences through which that "originating event" took possession of believers. Moreover, there are a number of points about the way the New Testament speaks of Jesus' resurrection that should be noted:

1) No individual or group is said to have witnessed the actual rising of Jesus.

2) The resurrection is never presented as a resuscitation; Jesus does not return to a former mode of earthly life (as Lazarus did, for example).

3) The Risen One is not immediately recognizable even to his closest associates. Though his risen body is in some way continuous with his earthly flesh, it is also decisively different, changed.

4) It is strongly implied that Jesus has entered God's presence (glory) in a new and definitive way; he has been "raised by God's glory" (Romans 6:4). Easter means God has somehow vindicated Jesus, has taken him into that future which Jesus himself had announced as "God's reign" (i.e., as God's self-bestowal, presence, grace, mercy and love).[67]

And that is not all. The New Testament seems convinced that *believers must experience the complex meanings of Easter for themselves.* The process by which this happens is *conversion.* The stories of Easter are above all stories of conversion, of disciples who recover from their previous doubt and depression, failure and flight. These experiences are often described in the New Testament as "seeing the Lord" (what scholars call the "appearance-story tradition";

e.g., Mary Magdalen at the tomb in John 20:11–18; the Emmaus journey in Luke 24:13–25; the breakfast at the seashore in John 21:1–14). Structurally all these stories have three features in common:

1) Each begins with a scene of doubt, disappointment, confusion or despair.

2) In each case, Jesus (initially unrecognized and treated as a stranger) takes the initiative, "explaining events," revealing his identity, eating and drinking with (or being touched by) others.

3) Each concludes with a scene of recognition ("Rabbouni!" "It is the Lord!" "Their eyes were opened and they recognized him").

The *seeing* involved in these stories is not so much a physical matter of gathering empirical evidence as it is an intuitive matter of grasping, understanding, and coming-to-believe ("Weren't our hearts burning within us as he spoke with us on the way and opened the scriptures?"). The appearances of Jesus are not so much "proofs" of the resurrection as "results," testaments of grace working in the disciples to open eyes and change hearts. To experience conversion, therefore, is to experience Easter. It is a process that is *gradual* (note how the disciples' moments of recognition follow periods of doubt and testing); *experienced as grace* (i.e., as God's initiative embodied in forgiveness of their previous failure and flight); *communal* (Jesus always appears to groups or, if appearing to individuals, gives the commission to "go and tell the others"); *linked, often, to the familiar gestures of a meal* (the disciples usually regroup around food and table, and "see Jesus" there).

As a collection of events, therefore, the Easter experience (God raising Jesus; the conversion of disciples, the grace of forgiveness, the beginnings of church) is seen in the New Testament as something altogether new. It is not the reappropriation or retrieval of the past. Easter does not reestablish the disciples' former relationship with Jesus but requires them to deal with someone—and something—new.

137

As a conversion experience, moreover, Easter draws the disciples toward the future. Recall how most of the appearance stories conclude with some kind of commissioning scene that defines the disciples' future activity (e.g., Matthew 28:16–20). *From now on, their experience of God and Jesus will be an experience of moving forward, with faith, into the future.* Easter thus represents the definitive crossing of what Sheehan calls "the eschatological line." Chronological conceptions of time give way to eschatological categories defined in terms of the only thing that matters—the total and immediate presence of God-with-humanity (the kind of presence into which Jesus, risen, has entered). The *past* is "the reign of sin and Satan, the alienation of people from God, the weight of all that [is] impenetrable to [God's] gift of self."[68] The *future* is God's gracious arrival at every moment of existence—forgiving, renewing, healing, making whole and raising up. This is the future into which Jesus was "raised by God's power," the future into which believers have been launched by baptism. And it is the future the community celebrates each time it gathers at table.

Miracles of Nature and Grace   In chapter two we saw that a central—and revolutionary—aspect of Jesus' ministry was his practice of "open commensality," i.e., his inclusive, egalitarian approach to table that welcomed anyone and everyone to feast abundantly in the name of "God's reign." There can be little doubt that after Easter the converted disciples confessed "Jesus' continued presence at the ritualized meals of the believing community."[69] The open commensality practiced during Jesus' life thus survived in the table tradition of the Christian assembly. As they gathered regularly to eat and drink, believers celebrated the "future present." Their table not only proclaimed the "death of the Lord" (1 Corinthians 11:26), but his resurrection—i.e., his "continuing presence in a continuing community," the "presence of the past Jesus in a radically new and transcendental mode of present and future existence."[70]

The connection between Easter experience and community eucharist is even clearer, scholars like Crossan suggest, if we look not only at Jesus' "table deeds" but at stories showing his power over nature (e.g., the multiplication of bread and fish; walking on water; and "fishing for humans" [linked in Luke 5:4–11 to a miraculous catch of fish]). These stories probably were "post-resurrectional" in origin and purpose; i.e., they were designed as dramatic demonstrations of the *Risen* Lord's presence and power in the believing community. Eventually, they also came to be connected with questions of community and leadership, power and authority, mission and mandate. (Crossan notes, for instance, that one can detect in these stories a trajectory that shows power moving steadily from *community-as-a-whole* to a *smaller leadership group*, to *specific individual leaders*."[71])

Here, however, our interest is in the way these stories illuminate the connection between Easter and eucharist. When we say "eucharist," of course, most of us automatically assume the centrality of that tradition which equates the sacramental elements of bread and wine with Christ's body and blood. It may startle us to discover that early Christian "eucharistic" art and iconography—as found, for instance in the catacombs—focused not on a meal of bread and wine (linked to a Last Supper scene) but on a meal of *bread and fish*. Indeed, there are no known depictions of the Last Supper (with bread-and-wine eucharist) in either catacomb or sarcophagus art. Instead, one finds, in paintings on the walls of the earliest Christian catacombs in Rome (dating from just before 200 CE), depictions of persons (usually seven or eleven in number, and presumably apostles) who are about to eat a meal of loaves and fishes. As Richard Hiers and Charles Kennedy conclude, in their study of such art,

> either for Jesus himself or for quite early, and probably, Jewish
> Christians, the meal of bread and fish, of which we learn in the

139

gospels, was understood as a eucharistic anticipation if not epiphanic participation in the blessed life of table-fellowship in the Kingdom of God.[72]

"What we are dealing with here," as John Crossan notes, "is the possibility of very early traditions about a resurrectional and ritualized meal of bread and fish involving Jesus and *the believing community as a whole,* that is, about the eucharistic presence of the Risen Lord but without any discriminating emphasis on leadership in general or on any one leader in particular."[73] For those of us accustomed to a eucharistic liturgy dominated by severely diminished symbols (tiny portions of bread and wine that scarcely suggest joyful abundance)—and by exaggerated concerns about the presider's authority, power and prestige—this may come as a shock. Indeed, it may have shocked some early Christians as well, for there is a clear tendency in several New Testament sources to suppress images of a "bread-and-fish banquet" in favor of an "Ultimate (Last) Supper" at which bread and wine are the focus, while *leaders alone* are present and (at least in Luke) are commissioned to repeat Jesus' actions.

I mention all this not to criticize our eucharistic traditions, but to show how very rich and diversified those traditions may originally have been. True, the paschal meal of the community proclaimed the *death* of Jesus, but it also proclaimed the joyful advent of God's reign, the exuberant abundance of a new creation, and the Risen Jesus' continued presence in a continuing community. Specialists in ritual studies, such as Catherine Bell, have shown that every community adopts strategies to help it distinguish *ritual* performance from other (and similar) ways of acting.[74] Among Christians this strategy seems to have resulted in a preference for distinguishing eucharist from other meals on a *quantitative* basis (ordinary meal = significant amounts of food; eucharistic meal = insignificant amounts of food, signaling that true nurture comes from God rather than from human effort or ingenuity).

Of course, the opposite strategy could have been adopted (abundant food as the symbol of God's extravagant liberality and graciousness)—and perhaps it was, in some early Christian circles. The point is that, when read in light of Easter and eucharist, the New Testament's "nature miracle" stories astonish us not because they suspend the laws of nature (through a sudden multiplication of loaves and fishes), but because they reveal how very rich, complex, subtle, surprising and generous the world's gifts already are—or can be. They force us to pay attention to what God is already, always doing in the world. They make us remember that the real miracle is the change that results from faith and conversion. They reveal that, despite all evidence to the contrary, the world is a place we can trust, a place where we can meet God. They show that in the unexpected bounty and pleasures of the table, the Risen One can be recognized.

In short, the story of loaves and fishes suggests that the eucharistic elements are meant to point to *abundance, generosity and openness* (the very things that characterized Jesus' open commensality). Note how Mark's treatment of this story (6:24–44) contrasts the joyful, compassionate generosity of Jesus with the grumbling stinginess and incomprehension of the disciples. They want Jesus to get rid of the crowd, to send them away hungry. (They also imply—but don't say outright—that the crowd consists of assorted strangers, trash and hangers-on, that it doesn't deserve care or attention.) Jesus brushes such objections aside and says simply: "Give them food." The disciples counter by complaining that it will cost too much (more than half a year's wages!). He replies, "Why don't you share some of the supplies you've secretly squirreled away?" (a somewhat sarcastic comment, since the disciples were expected to carry *nothing* on their missionary journey—no food, no sack, no money [6:8]—but instead to rely on the kindness of strangers to provide food and shelter). Caught red-handed, the disciples grudgingly admit they have five loaves and two fish. Then Jesus creates a dinner of luxurious abundance—the whole crowd reclining on a carpet of soft, green grass; the food plentiful; the leftovers substantial.

This is a scene and story especially worth considering today, when we are still suffering from centuries of a sacramental minimalism that has stressed efficacy and causality at the expense of signification.[75] We still need to open up our symbols so they can be experienced as rich, full, hearty and generous. We need water that bubbles, swirls, rushes, splashes, rises and falls—water you can bathe in, immerse yourself in. We need fragrant oil that pours, flows, glides and glistens, generously, over human bodies. And we need bread and wine that evoke, by their very heartiness, fragrance and flavor, nature's bountiful fertility—thereby symbolizing the nurturing, inexhaustible presence of the Risen One.

We can see, too, why the *General Introduction* to Christian initiation correctly links the neophytes' sharing of eucharist at the Easter Vigil with their participation in the priesthood of Jesus and the mission of the church.[76]

The "nature miracle" stories (such as Mark's account of "loaves and fishes") imply that *eating and drinking the eucharist is a pledge to feed the world*—to feed it generously, compassionately, fearlessly, indiscriminately, without judgment. Note again how Mark's dramatic story unfolds. The disciples react to human need by complaining and calculating, by whining that indiscriminate generosity will imperil their own future. But Jesus rejects all such excuses, insisting that *if you give all you have, you will find that there is more than enough for everyone.*

The eucharist thus enacts and embodies not only the death of Jesus and the presence of the Risen One, but the community's generous and compassionate response to human need. It is not only a miracle of nature (abundant food for the hungry) but a miracle of grace (conversion and faith— even for the grumbling disciples of Mark's story!). In the midst of the meal Jesus is present not as some imperious poobah—giving orders, turning the "nobodies" away—but as the servant who stoops with basin and towel in hand to wash the feet of all.

"Why Do You Seek the Living among the Dead?"

The theology of Easter (exemplified by "nature miracle" stories like that of the loaves and fishes) has illumined our understanding of eucharist by showing that the Christian meal is meant to symbolize the generous, abundant, joyful feasting in the kingdom of God that Jesus embodied at a table that was compassionate, inclusive, egalitarian and open to strangers. The implication is that, for Christians, the practice of open commensality ("doing as Jesus did") *is/becomes/constitutes* the very experience of the Risen One's presence and power. That is why eucharist brings the sacraments of Christian initiation to their completion. Having been washed, anointed and sealed with the Spirit, neophytes are led into the eucharistic assembly, where they exercise their priesthood by participating in the most radical act of the church's mission, the act in which the church literally follows its Savior's lead: Bread-breakers become bread broken; the diners become the world's dinner; the body *at* the table becomes the body *on* the table. For the life of the world.

But there is also another insight into eucharist that the Easter mystery offers. It has to do with the "seeking" that all the New Testament accounts mention in connection with the empty tomb: "Do not be afraid! I know you are seeking Jesus the crucified" (Matthew 28:5); "Why do you seek the living one among the dead?" (Luke 24:5); "Woman, why are you weeping? Whom are you seeking?" (John 20:15). In its origins, these texts imply, Easter has something essential to do with seeking—indeed, is inseparable from it. As Thomas Sheehan has noted, the New Testament strongly hints that Easter " 'happens' only to those who seek it. At the origin of Easter we find not a past historical event but an ongoing hermeneutical task."[77]

Seeking, of course, makes sense only if something—or someone—is absent. At the same time, our very act of seeking implies that the object of our search can be found and known:

> No one seeks for what is already present and is known as such. But on the other hand, no one can search for what is totally absent, entirely unknown or unknowable. . . . What makes the seeking possible is something sought-for which is absent but not totally absent. All seeking is initiated and guided by the absent as seekable, something desired but not possessed, something guessed at but not fully known, something partially present in its absence.[78]

In the New Testament, significantly, it is women who are Easter's primary seekers. Their seeking begins, sorrowfully, as the search for someone so loved that life seems impossible without him—someone now lost and gone forever,

> someone good, whose goodness never became a burden to others;
> someone who called the impenetrable riddle that lies behind all things "Abba";
> someone who really knew something but was never abstruse when speaking about it;
> someone who could show you the ultimate scheme of things and your place at the center of it;
> someone who woke you out of the pettiness of the everyday and led you beyond yourself;
> someone you could dare to hold and touch and kiss;
> someone who sought nothing for himself;
> someone who let you know that God—your God—was arriving and would live with you forever;
> someone who made everything physically present to you: God's pity, grace and nearness.[79]

For the spice-bearing women at Jesus' tomb, "mourning *is* their search—their way of living into an absence that is excruciatingly present precisely because the absent loved one is *not*."[80]

These women at the tomb have something essential to teach us about both Easter and eucharist. They tell us that the meaning of both experiences is rooted not in control, possession and holding on, but in seeking, surrender and letting go. They tell us of a kind of *seeking that takes us from tomb to table.* For the women come to the tomb seeking the One whom they feel they cannot live without; and they expect to find a body—a corpse they can tenderly caress, anoint with spices and perfume, and wrap in scented linen. Instead, they find nothing. Not only is Jesus dead, even his body has disappeared. The women's seeking is doubly frustrated: no living Jesus to comfort them, no corpse to care for. The absence is absolute; the tomb is empty.

At this point, two reactions are possible: rage or redefinition. Rage sustains the illusion of control; it encourages belief that anger—expressed long enough, hard enough, and to the right people—can change things (can coax a robber to return Jesus' body, can coax God to relent and let him live again). Anger bargains, rage blackmails. Redefinition, however, surrenders to the absence, the emptiness; it fully embraces the experience of seeking (futile and fruitless as it might appear to be). Rage keeps seekers at the tomb, bargaining; redefinition leads them away, back to town and table. The women chose to let themselves be redefined by their desire, to surrender fully to their seeking. They chose unrestricted desire—however painful and unfulfilled—as essential to their human identity. And they thus opened up that option to us as well. For,

As we peer into that emptiness, the absence of the living Jesus and even of his dead body allows us to identify a unique form of seeking: the desire for that which can never be had. This unique kind of seeking is the experience that makes human beings different from any other kind of entity, and we see it exemplified in the women who actually found the tomb empty on the first Easter Sunday. *Such seeking is not something we occasionally get caught up in; rather, it is what makes us human, constitutes us as the futile passion, the unfulfilled and presumably unfulfillable desire that we are.* If we were not this endless *eros,* either we would be God, who cannot seek because God has already found everything, or we would be animals, those living entities that lack an "ontological imagination" and therefore

145

never have a desire that exceeds the possibility of being fulfilled. . . .

We remain, fundamentally, an act of questioning to which there is no answer . . . this endless and unfulfillable seeking.[81]

It is precisely this experience (this *redefinition*) of ourselves as unrestricted desire, as unfulfillable longing, as unanswered question, that constitutes our experience of the Risen One. For desire and seeking are what move us from tomb to table, from Easter to eucharist. The women had the right response. They stood for a time in fear, traumatized and amazed—then, saying nothing to anyone (Mark 16:8), they took the path that led away from the tomb, back to town, back to their own lives, back to denials and doubts, affirmations and taxes, the holy canons of madrigal, the mandates of touch. They returned not to what Jesus *was,* but to what Jesus *was about:* the presence of God in the troubling textures of ordinary life, the presence of the Holy One in the smoking fire, the spit of fat in the pan, the baking of bread, the pressing of grape, the making of meals. The women tell us where our desire must turn, where our seeking must take us—from Sunday to Sunday, from Easter to Easter. *To eucharist.* Not simply to eucharist as rite, but to eucharist as existence.

Perhaps as the women turned back toward town, they were singing this song:

I look for you, I look for your image among the medals
that the gray sky models and abandons,
I do not know who you are but I owe you so much
that the earth is filled with my bitter treasure.
What salt, what geography, what stone does not lift
its secret banner from what it was shielding?
What leaf on falling was not for me a long book
of words addressed and loved by someone? . . .
You are, you are perhaps, the man or the woman
or the tenderness that deciphered nothing.
Or perhaps you did not clutch the dark human
firmament, the throbbing star, perhaps
on treading you did not know that from the blind earth
comes forth the ardent day of steps that seek you.[82]

Endnotes

Chapter 1

[1] Flannery O'Connor, *The Complete Stories* (New York: Farrar, Straus and Giroux, 1971).

[2] Thomas Sheehan, *The First Coming: How the Kingdom of God Became Christianity* (New York: Random House Vintage Books, 1988), 61.

[3] John Dominic Crossan, *The Historical Jesus: The Life of a Mediterranean Jewish Peasant* (San Francisco: Harper-Collins, 1991), xxvi.

[4] W. H. Gardner, ed., *Poems of Gerard Manley Hopkins* (New York: Oxford University Press, 1948), 112.

[5] Sheehan, *The First Coming,* 63.

[6] Ibid., 67.

[7] Thomas H. Johnson, ed., *The Complete Poems of Emily Dickinson* (Boston: Little, Brown & Company, 1960), 116.

[8] See R. Funk, B. Scott, J. Butts, eds., *The Parables of Jesus: Red Letter Edition* (Sonoma CA: Polebridge Press, 1988).

[9] See Bernard B. Scott, *Jesus, Symbol-Maker for the Kingdom* (Philadelphia: Fortress Press, 1981), 30–32, 115–20.

[10] Ibid., 31, emphasis added.

[11] O'Connor, *The Complete Stories,* 131.

[12] Ibid., 132.

[13] Scott, *Jesus, Symbol-Maker,* 117.

[14] Sheehan, *The First Coming,* 225.

[15] Crossan, *The Historical Jesus,* 281.

[16] Bernard B. Scott, *Hear Then the Parable A Commentary on the Parables of Jesus* (Minneapolis: Fortress Press, 1989), 328–29.

[17] Philo of Alexandria, *Legum Allegoria,* (= Philo I; Loeb Classical Library 226), trans. F. H. Colson and G. H. Whitaker (Cambridge: Harvard University Press, 1956), 352–53.

[18] O'Connor, *The Complete Stories,* 497.

[19] Ibid., 499.

[20] Ibid., 500, emphasis added.

[21] Ibid., 507.

[22] Ibid., 508–9, emphasis added.

[23] Scott, *Jesus, Symbol-Maker,* 119.

[24] Michael J. Cormack, *Ideology* (Ann Arbor MI: The University of Michigan Press, 1992), 16.

[25] For the probable version in Jesus' preaching, see Funk, Scott, Butts, *The Parables of Jesus,* 42–43.

[26]Scott, *Hear Then,* 173–74, emphasis added.

[27]O'Connor, *The Complete Stories,* 447.

[28]Ibid., 480.

[29]Ibid., 481, emphasis added.

[30]Ibid., 482.

[31]Ibid., 482.

[32]Dan Otto Via, *The Parables: Their Literary and Existential Dimension* (Philadelphia: Fortress Press, 1967), 96.

[33]Via, *The Parables,* 97.

[34]Robert W. Funk, *Parables and Presence: Forms of the New Testament Tradition* (Philadelphia: Fortress Press, 1982), 130.

[35]Funk, *Parables and Presence,* 132.

[36]Stanley Hopper, *Interpretation: The Poetry of Meaning* (New York: Harcourt, Brace & World, 1967), xix.

[37]Funk, *Parables and Presence,* 131.

[38]Ibid., 131–32.

[39]Norman Perrin, *Rediscovering the Teaching of Jesus* (New York: Harper & Row, 1967), 103.

[40]Igor de Garine, "Food, Tradition and Prestige," in *Food, Man & Society,* ed. D. N. Walcher et al. (New York: Plenum Press, 1976), 150, emphasis added.

[41]de Garine, "Food, Tradition," 150.

[42]Lee Edward Klosinski, *The Meals in Mark,* (Ann Arbor MI: University Microfilms International, 1988), 205.

[43]Klosinski, *The Meals in Mark,* 206.

[44]Sheehan, *The First Coming,* 72.

[45]Karl Rahner, "On Christian Dying," trans. D. Bourke, in *Theological Investigations,* vol VII (New York: Herder & Herder, 1971), 287.

[46]Rahner, "On Christian Dying," 289.

[47]Ibid., 290.

[48]Gardner, *Poems of Gerard Manley Hopkins,* 70.

[49]Edith Sitwell, *The Canticle of the Rose: Poems 1917–1949,* (New York: Vanguard, 1949), 238.

[50]Karl Rahner and Herbert Vorgrimler, *Theological Dictionary,* ed. C. Ernst, trans. R. Strachan (New York: Herder & Herder, 1965), 118.

[51]Karl Rahner, "Theological Considerations Concerning the Moment of Death," trans. D. Bourke, in *Theological Investigations,* vol. XI (New York: Seabury, 1974), 320–21, emphasis added.

[52]Perrin, *Rediscovering,* 103.

[53]Ibid., 107–8.

[54]Doris Donnelly, "Ambassadors of Reconciliation," *Weavings* 5 (January/February 1990): 18–19.

[55]Herbert Fingarette, *Confucius—The Secular as Sacred* (New York: Harper & Row, 1972), 1–17.

[56]Margaret Visser, *The Rituals of Dinner* (New York: Grove Weidenfeld, 1991), 22, 23.

[57]Gabe Huck and Mary Ann Simcoe, eds., *A Triduum Sourcebook* (Chicago: Liturgy Training Publications, 1983), 111, text adapted, emphasis added.

[58]Pierre Teilhard de Chardin, *Hymn of the Universe,* trans. Gerald Vann (New York: Harper & Row, 1969), 23–24, 34, text adapted.

Chapter 2

[1]Aidan Kavanagh, *The Shape of Baptism* (New York: Pueblo, 1978), 122, emphasis added.

[2]Kavanagh, *The Shape of Baptism,* 176–77.

[3]Gail Ramshaw, *Words Around the Fire* (Chicago: Liturgy Training Publications, 1990), 76.

[4]V. de Sola Pinto and W. Roberts, eds., *The Complete Poems of D. H. Lawrence,* vol. II (New York: Viking, 1964), 728.

[5]Richard Leakey, *Origins* (New York: Dutton, 1977), 151–52, emphasis added.

[6]Diane Ackerman, *A Natural History of the Senses* (New York: Random House, 1990), 172.

[7]Kavanagh, *The Shape of Baptism,* 160.

[8]Joachim Jeremias, *Jerusalem in the Time of Jesus,* trans. F. H. and C. H. Cave (Philadelphia: Fortress Press, 1969), 27.

[9]Zeno of Verona, *Tractatus,* vol. 22 of *Corpus Christianorum,* ed. B. Lefstedt (Turnholt: Brepols, 1971), 51, my translation.

[10]Ackerman, *A Natural History,* 129.

[11]Ibid., 130.

[12]Pablo Neruda, *Residence on Earth,* trans. Donald D. Walsh (New York: New Directions, 1973), 161.

[13]David Gilmore, "Anthropology of the Mediterranean Area," *Annual Review of Anthropology* 11 (1982): 192.

[14]Gilmore, "Anthropology," 178–79.

[15]Andrew J. Overman, "Who Were the First Urban Christians?" in *Society of Biblical Literature Seminar Papers,* ed. D. Lull (Atlanta: Scholars Press, 1988), no. 27: 165–68.

[16]Jane Schneider, "Of Vigilance and Virgins: Honor, Shame and Access to Resources in Mediterranean Societies," *Ethnology* 9 (1971): 2–3, emphasis added.

[17]Ibid., 3.

[18]Ibid., 2, emphasis added.

[19]Ibid., 3.

[20]Ibid., 2, emphasis added.

[21]Gilmore, "Anthropology," 191.

[22]John Dominic Crossan, *The Historical Jesus The Life of a Mediterranean Jewish Peasant* (San Francisco: Harper Collins, 1991), 10–11.

[23]Schneider, "Of Vigilance," 18.

[24]Ibid., 20.

[25] Gilmore, "Anthropology," 195.

[26] Crossan, *The Historical Jesus*, 15.

[27] Gilmore, "Anthropology," 192.

[28] Ibid., 193.

[29] Crossan, *The Historical Jesus*, 59.

[30] Ibid., 62–63.

[31] Ibid., 60–61.

[32] Gilmore, "Anthropology," 193.

[33] Bruce Malina and Jerome Neyrey, *Calling Jesus Names: The Social Value of Labels in Matthew* (Sonoma CA: Polebridge Press, 1988), 145–51.

[34] Dennis Smith and Hal Taussig, *Many Tables The Eucharist in the New Testament and Liturgy Today* (Philadelphia: Trinity Press International, 1990), 22.

[35] Smith and Taussig, *Many Tables*, 24. Also cf. John 13:23.

[36] See Dennis Smith, "Social Obligation in the Context of Communal Meals: A Study of the Christian Meal in 1 Corinthians in Comparison with Graeco-Roman Communal Meals" (Th.D. diss., Harvard University Press, 1980), 20.

[37] Mary Douglas, "Deciphering a Meal," *Daedalus* 101 (1972): 61.

[38] Smith, "Social Obligation," 29.

[39] Smith and Taussig, *Many Tables*, 33.

[40] Roland Barthes, "A Psychosociology of Contemporary Food Consumption," in *Food and Drink in History*, ed. R. Forster and O. Ranum (Baltimore: Johns Hopkins University Press, 1979), 172–78. Referenced in Lee Edward Klosinski, *The Meals in Mark* (Ann Arbor MI: University Microfilms International, 1988), note 56.

[41] Klosinski, *The Meals in Mark*, 56–58, emphasis added.

[42] Crossan, *The Historical Jesus*, 422.

[43] Thomas Sheehan, *The First Coming: How the Kingdom of God Became Christianity* (New York: Random House Vintage Books, 1988), 61.

[44] Leif Eric Vaage, *Q: The Ethos and Ethics of an Itinerant Intelligence* (Ann Arbor MI: University of Microfilms International, 1987), 374–75.

[45] Crossan, *The Historical Jesus*, 83–88.

[46] Ibid., 360.

[47] Mary Douglas, *Purity and Danger: An Analysis of Concepts of Pollution and Taboo* (New York: Praeger, 1966), 35.

[48] Malina and Neyrey, *Calling Jesus Names*, 37.

[49] Crossan, *The Historical Jesus*, 324, emphasis added.

[50] George Hunsinger, "Jesus and the Leper," *Weavings* 5 (1990): 32–33.

[51] Ibid., 35.

[52] Crossan, *The Historical Jesus*, 341.

[53] Ibid., 341.

[54] Ibid., 344.

[55] Ibid., 262, 263.

[56] Geza Vermes, *The Dead Sea Scrolls in English,* rev. ed. (Baltimore: Penguin Books, 1968), 121, translation altered.

[57] Crossan, *The Historical Jesus,* 404, emphasis added.

[58] Klosinski, *The Meals in Mark,* 199–200.

[59] Robert M. Fowler, *Loaves and Fishes: The Function of the Feeding Stories in the Gospel of Mark,* no. 54 of Society of Biblical Literature Dissertation Series (Chico CA: Scholars Press, 1981), 137.

[60] Ibid., 138.

[61] Ibid., 147.

[62] Smith, "Social Obligation," 2.

[63] Dennis Smith, "Table Fellowship as a Literary Motif in the Gospel of Luke," *Journal of Biblical Literature* 106 (1987): 638.

[64] E. P. Sanders, *Jesus and Judaism* (Philadelphia: Fortress Press, 1985), 187.

[65] Klosinski, *The Meals in Mark,* 212, emphasis added.

[66] Fowler, *Loaves and Fishes,* 132.

[67] Klosinski, *The Meals in Mark,* 176.

[68] Ibid., 202.

[69] Ibid., 120.

[70] Cited in Crossan, *The Historical Jesus,* 366–67.

Chapter 3

[1] Lee Edward Klosinski, *The Meals in Mark* (Ann Arbor MI: University Microfilms International, 1988), 205.

[2] Aidan Kavanagh, *The Shape of Baptism* (New York: Pueblo, 1978), 108.

[3] Ibid., 108.

[4] Austin Flannery, ed., *Vatican Council II: The Conciliar and Post Conciliar Documents* (Collegeville: The Liturgical Press, 1975), 14–15.

[5] Ibid., 161–62, slightly altered.

[6] Karl Rahner and Herbert Vorgrimler, *Theological Dictionary,* ed. C. Ernst, trans. R. Strachan (New York: Herder & Herder, 1965), 155.

[7] Michael Skelley, *The Liturgy of the World Karl Rahner's Theology of Worship* (Collegeville: The Liturgical Press, 1991), 147.

[8] Kavanagh, *The Shape of Baptism,* 107.

[9] "Preparing and Celebrating the Paschal Feasts," #90–91, *Origins* 17 (March 17, 1988): 685.

[10] General Introduction to Christian Initiation, #2 in *Rite of Christian Initiation of Adults* (Chicago: Liturgy Training Publications, 1988), xiv, emphasis added.

[11] Annie Dillard, *Pilgrim at Tinker Creek* (New York: Bantam Books, 1975), 278–79, emphasis added.

[12] Austin Flannery, ed., "Decree on the Apostolate of Lay People," #6 in *Vatican Council II: The Conciliar and Post Conciliar Documents* (Collegeville: The Liturgical Press), 772, emphasis added.

[13]"Decree on the Church's Missionary Activity," #15, slightly altered. Excerpted in *Rite of Christian Initiation of Adults* (Chicago: Liturgy Training Publications, 1988), 372.

[14]Kathleen Raine, *Collected Poems 1935–1980* (London: Allen & Unwin, 1981), 35–37.

[15]Karl Rahner, "Considerations on the Active Role of the Person in the Sacramental Event," trans. D. Bourke, in *Theological Investigations*, vol. XIV (New York: Seabury, 1976), 169–70.

[16]Karl Rahner, "On the Theology of Worship," trans. E. Quinn, in *Theological Investigations*, vol. XIX (New York: Crossroad, 1983), 142.

[17]Ibid., 142–43.

[18]Ibid., 143, text slightly altered.

[19]Ibid., 143.

[20]Ben Belitt, trans., *Selected Poems of Pablo Neruda* (New York: Grove Press, 1961), 39.

[21]Rahner, "On the Theology," 147.

[22]Skelley, *The Liturgy of the World,* 75.

[23]Rahner, "On the Theology," 148.

[24]Pablo Neruda, "Unity," in *Residence on Earth,* trans. Donald D. Walsh (New York: New Directions, 1973), 15.

[25]Neruda, *Residence,* 153.

[26]Skelley, *The Liturgy of the World,* 81–82.

[27]See Karl Rahner, "Considerations on the Active Role," 166, 169.

[28]*Rite of Christian Initiation of Adults* (Chicago: Liturgy Training Publications, 1988), #244.

[29]Neruda, *Residence,* 181.

[30]Thomas Traherne, *Centuries, Poems and Thanksgivings* (Oxford: Clarendon Press, 1958), 11, 14, 15.

[31]Neruda, *Residence,* 157.

[32]Pierre Teilhard de Chardin, *How I Believe,* trans. R. Hague (San Francisco: Harper & Row, 1969), 3.

[33]See Harvey Egan, *An Anthology of Christian Mysticism* (Collegeville: The Liturgical Press, 1991), 559.

[34]"The Mystical Milieu," cited in Egan, *Anthology,* 570–71.

[35]Karl Rahner, "The Festival of the Future of the World," trans. D. Bourke, in *Theological Investigations,* vol. VII (New York: Seabury, 1977), 183–84.

[36]Ibid., 184.

[37]Dillard, *Pilgrim at Tinker Creek,* 33–34.

[38]Leonard Cohen, *Book of Mercy* (New York: Villard, 1984), 89, slightly altered.

[39]Parker Palmer, *The Company of Strangers* (New York: Crossroad, 1981), 22–29.

[40]Ibid., 118–34.

[41]Ibid., 22.

[42]Ibid., 23.

[43]Richard Sennett, *The Fall of Public Man* (New York: Knopf, 1977), 259.

[44]Palmer, *The Company of Strangers,* 24.

[45]Ibid., 119.

[46]Ibid., 120.

[47]Aidan Kavanagh, "Liturgical Inculturation: Looking to the Future," *Studia Liturgica* 20:1 (1990): 102.

[48]Ibid., 102.

[49]Palmer, *The Company of Strangers,* 126.

[50]Ibid., 132.

[51]Ibid., 121.

[52]Ibid., 121.

[53]Robert Bellah, "Liturgy and Experience," in *The Roots of Ritual,* ed. J. D. Shaughnessy (Grand Rapids MI: Eerdmans, 1973), 230, emphasis added.

[54]Herman Melville, *Moby Dick* (New York: Harper & Brothers, 1950), 124.

[55]Belah, "Liturgy and Experience," 231.

[56]Ibid., 232.

[57]Ibid., 233–34.

[58]*Rite of Christian Initiation of Adults,* #8.

[59]RCIA, #12.

[60]RCIA, #17.

[61]RCIA, #23.

[62]RCIA, #26.

[63]RCIA, #207.

[64]Daniel J. Sheerin, *The Eucharist,* vol. 7 of *Message of the Fathers of the Church* (Wilmington DE: Michael Glazier, 1986), 95, emphasis added.

[65]ICEL, trans., *The Liturgy of the Hours* (New York: Catholic Book Publishing Co., 1975), vol. II, 583, altered.

[66]Ibid., 661, emphasis added.

[67]See Joseph Fitzmyer, *A Christological Catechism,* 2d ed. (New York: Paulist Press, 1991), 90–93.

[68]Sheehan, *The First Coming,* 66.

[69]Crossan, *The Historical Jesus,* 402.

[70]Ibid., 404.

[71]Ibid., 398.

[72]R. H. Hiers and C. A. Kennedy, "The Bread and Fish Eucharist in the Gospels and Early Christian Art," *Perspectives in Religious Studies* 3 (1976): 45.

[73]Crossan, *The Historical Jesus,* 399.

[74]See Catherine Bell, "Ritual, Change and Changing Rituals," *Worship* 63 (1989): 35–36.

[75]See Bishops' Committee on the Liturgy, *Environment and Art in Catholic Worship* (Washington DC: National Conference of Catholic Bishops, 1978), #14.

[76]General Introduction, #2, in *Rite of Christian Initiation of Adults,* xiv.

[77]Sheehan, *The First Coming,* 167.

[78]Ibid., 167–68.

[79]Adapted from Rahner, "The Festival," 182 and Sheehan, *The First Coming,* 170.

ENDNOTES

[80]Sheehan, *The First Coming*, 168, emphasis added.

[81]Ibid., 172, emphasis added.

[82]Neruda, *Residence*, 225.